Bloom's

GUIDES

Chaim Potok's
The Chosen

CURRENTLY AVAILABLE

1984
The Adventures of Huckleberry Finn
All the Pretty Horses
Beloved
Brave New World
The Chosen
The Crucible
Cry, the Beloved Country
Death of a Salesman
The Grapes of Wrath
Great Expectations
Hamlet
The Handmaid's Tale
The House on Mango Street
I Know Why the Caged Bird Sings
The Iliad
Lord of the Flies
Macbeth
Maggie: A Girl of the Streets
The Member of the Wedding
Pride and Prejudice
Ragtime
Romeo and Juliet
The Scarlet Letter
Snow Falling on Cedars
A Streetcar Named Desire
The Things They Carried
To Kill a Mockingbird

Bloom's

GUIDES

Chaim Potok's
The Chosen

Edited & with an Introduction
by Harold Bloom

CHELSEA HOUSE
PUBLISHERS
A Haights Cross Communications Company

Philadelphia

A Haights Cross Communications ✦ Company

www.chelseahouse.com

Introduction © 2005 by Harold Bloom.

First Printing
1 3 5 7 9 8 6 4 2

Library of Congress Cataloging-in-Publication Data
Chaim Potoi's The Chosen/Harold Bloom, editor
   p.cm.—(Bloom's guides)
  Includes bibliographical references and index.
  ISBN: 0-7910-8173-7 (alk. paper)
1. Potok, Chaim. Chosen. 2. Brooklyn (New York, NY.Y.)—literature.
3. Fathers and sons in literature. 4. Teenage boys in literature. 5. Jews in literature. I. Bloom, Harold. II. Series.
  PS3566.O69C54 2004
  813'.54—dc22

                    2004013704

Contributing editor: Jenn McKee
Cover design by Takeshi Takahashi
Layout by EJB Publishing Services

Contents

Introduction

HAROLD BLOOM

I read Chaim Potok's *The Chosen* when it appeared, in 1967, when I was thirty-seven. Half-a-lifetime later, soon to be seventy-four, I have just reread the book. What was poignant then is still touching; what was mawkish seems to me even more awkward. Period pieces, when they aspire to literature, can survive for two generations or so, but not longer. By chance I have also just read a proof-copy of Philip Roth's newest novel, *The Plot Against America*. Potok is obliterated by juxtaposition with Roth, but I do not mean to be unfair. Roth is a major writer, author of such permanent splendors as *American Pastoral* and *Sabbath's Theater*, comparable to the best of Thomas Pynchon, Cormac McCarthy and Don DeLillo. Among American Jewish novelists, Roth is challenged only by Nathanael West. Saul Bellow and Bernard Malamud, admirable authors, seem to me a rung below. Potok clearly is another phenomenon, akin to popular writers like Herman Wouk and Leon Uris. I prefer liberal and humane period pieces like *The Chosen* to nasty ones like Ayn Rand's *The Fountainhead*, but that expresses only my personal affiliations, and not my critical stance or function, as I conceive such matters.

The Chosen, like most period pieces, was fortunately timed: the Counter-culture, which now has become our official media and academic culture, repelled hundreds of thousands of readers, Christians and Jews, who preferred more traditional morals and manners. Though Potok rather weirdly gave credit to Evelyn Waugh's *Brideshead Revisited* as his immediate inspiration, *The Chosen* actually imitates Hemingway's style and modes of characterization. There is a curious gap between Potok's spiritual allegiances and subject matter, and his popularization of Hemingway's art.

Potok, despite Hemingway's example, never learned to write believable dialogue, and his characters always remained mere names upon the page. His appeal was and remains, for a while longer anyway, an invitation to study the nostalgias of an earlier time, the United States of 1945–65. I myself participate in some aspects of those nostalgias but I cannot recommend a rereading of *The Chosen*.

Biographical Sketch

Herman Harold Potok, born February 17, 1929 in the Bronx, received a Hebrew name by which he is better known: Chaim, which means "life"—an appropriate moniker for an optimist who spent much of his time writing life-affirming stories, essays, and novels about Jewish life in America.

Years before his birth, Chaim's Orthodox father, Benjamin Max Potok, immigrated to America from Poland. After fighting alongside other Poles against the Russians during World War I, Benjamin returned to Poland to find Jews facing pogroms (the organized persecution of Jews), so he came to the Bronx and pursued a career first as a stationery salesman, and then, following the Depression, as a jeweler and watchmaker.

Mollie Friedman, Chaim's mother, an ultra-Orthodox Polish Jew who had also fled her home country, met and married Benjamin. And although Benjamin eschewed the traditional garb—earlocks, beard, cords—he considered himself a Hasid; thus, Potok grew up in a highly strict, deeply religious environment (not unlike that of *The Chosen*'s Danny Saunders). Indeed, Potok's family prioritized religion to such a great degree that not only did Potok himself receive a rabbinical ordination, but his brother also became a rabbi, and his two sisters married rabbis.

Because Potok was born at the time of the Great Depression, his surroundings were rife with poverty and occasionally dangerous. After the stock market crash, many working class Jews in the Potoks' neighborhood lost their jobs, and because they shared neighborhoods with other poor ethnic groups—Italians, Polish, Irish, African-Americans—the economic tensions sometimes evolved into racial/ethnic hatred and violence. The Potoks, like so many at that time, had to go on welfare.

And although this likely caused great discomfort and anxiety within the family, nothing could match the horror of Jewish genocide in Europe. The Holocaust haunted Potok's work throughout his career, not surprisingly, as consumed by these fears as he had been as a child.

Potok's artistic gifts initially manifested themselves in the visual arts. At age nine, he already had a knack for both painting and drawing (thus providing him, much later, with material for two Asher Lev novels). His culture, however, did not encourage this passion, believing that the time and effort spent on such trifles detracted from studying religious texts, the word of God. As a result, Potok often pointed out in interviews, there is little to no Jewish tradition in the visual arts.

Although Potok's artistic pursuits were merely dismissed as superfluous when he was a child, they assumed darker, more malevolent tones after his bar mitzvah. His community then deemed his interests as sinister and morally repugnant, causing much tense conflict and anxiety within his family. Teenaged Potok soon found a different sort of inspiration, though, in the form of Evelyn Waugh's book, *Brideshead Revisited*. Though the novel about a rich English Catholic family wouldn't necessarily seem the most obvious artistic point of origin for Potok, it addressed one of the author's primary thematic concerns: how does one take part in the secular, humanist American culture while still staying true to one's religious and/or ethnic background?

To further explore such questions, among others, Potok read Ernest Hemingway, William Faulkner, Thomas Mann, and, significantly, James Joyce's *Portrait of the Artist as a Young Man* while a student at the Talmudic Academy High School of Yeshiva University, in Manhattan's Washington Heights neighborhood. Together, these books convinced him to turn his creative energies toward writing. Eventually, however, Potok's community expressed the same reservations about creative writing as they had visual arts, and this eventually led Potok, while in college, to turn away from his Hasidic roots and embrace the less rigid lifestyle of a Conservative Jew. The move, naturally, was difficult; Potok once said, "It wrenched my world entirely. I lost all of my friends. I lost most of my teachers. I had to literally reconstruct my existence" (Walden viii). It's not at all surprising, then, that Potok's main theme was often the inherent conflicts that exist between Orthodox Jewry and American values.

Graduating with a B.A. in English literature, summa cum laude, in 1950 from Yeshiva University—contributing short stories and articles to the yearbook, of which he became editor along the way—Potok went on to study for the Conservative Jewish rabbinate at the Jewish Theological Seminary of America, in New York City. After achieving great academic success, and winning some of the school's most prestigious prizes, he received his smicha, or rabbinic ordination, in 1954. Soon, though, he volunteered to be a combat chaplain in Korea, serving from 1955–57. The experience affected him more than any other, changing his perspective about humanity while serving soldiers of various faiths. (This led him to write two of his later works, *The Book of Lights* and *I Am the Clay*, as well as his first attempt at a novel, a manuscript that was never published.)

Upon returning to the United States, Potok decided to pursue a career in education. From 1957–59, he taught at the University of Judaism while also running a year-round Conservative Jewish camp in Los Angeles. While working at Camp Ramah, Potok met a social worker named (Adena) Sarah Mosevitzky, and they soon married. Intellectually, though, Potok soon grew restless and decided to pursue a doctorate in philosophy at the University of Pennsylvania; to this end, he and Sarah moved to Philadelphia in 1959. Three years later, Sarah gave birth to a daughter, Rena, in 1962.

After living with his family for a year in Israel—to work on his dissertation about Solomon Maimon, a rebellious Jewish intellectual who was clearly a model for *The Chosen*'s Danny Saunders—Potok moved his family, in 1964, back to Brooklyn, where Hasidic communities lived; this gave him more access again to their isolated world, which had always been a point of fascination for him.

Adena gave birth to a second daughter, Naama, in 1965, which coincided with the time that Potok received his doctorate. Soon, he assumed a position as editor in chief for the Jewish Publication Society of America, and in 1967, he published his first novel, *The Chosen*, to great acclaim.

In 1968, Adena gave birth to their last child, a son named

Akiva, while Potok pursued the writing of a sequel to *The Chosen*, titled *The Promise* (1969), which was also well-received. And significant to his interest in the visual arts, Potok published *My Name is Asher Lev* in 1972, which chronicled the evolution of a conflicted Jewish artist who feels caught between his talent and the strictures of his religion.

Potok, who found he felt no longer welcome among the Hasids but also not wholly comfortable among Conservative Jews, moved his family back to Israel in 1973. After four years—during which time Potok published the novel *In the Beginning* (1975)—the family returned to the Philadelphia area, where Potok lived for the remainder of his life.

In 1978, Potok released his first non-fiction work, *Wanderings: Chaim Potok's History of the Jews*, which strove to provide a personal, accessible, and scholarly account of Jewish history. The experience of writing the book deeply affected him, and this manifested itself in the turn his fiction took at this time. *The Book of Lights* (1981), for instance, dealt with Jewish mysticism and concerned one man's study of the Kabbalah as a way to make meaning of evil's coexistence with goodness in the world.

The 1980s and 1990s witnessed Potok accepting temporary teaching positions at various colleges (Penn, Bryn Mawr, Johns Hopkins), but he never stopped publishing. *Davita's Harp* (1985), his sixth novel, marked a significant departure for Potok, in that it focused on a female character; his previous work often only featured highly marginalized female characters, emphasizing instead the relationships between fathers and sons, and men in general.

In 1990, Potok published *The Gift of Asher Lev*, a sequel, and in 1992, he published *I Am the Clay*, a story focusing on a Korean family caught in the crossfire of war. In 1996, though, Potok returned to more familiar territory when he published *The Gates of November: Chronicles of the Slepak Family*. The non-fiction work recounted the story of a Jewish family who escaped Russian and Soviet persecution.

The nineties also witnessed Potok trying his hand at playwriting (*Out of the Depths, Sins of the Father, The Play of*

Lights, and an adaptation of *The Chosen*) and children's literature (*The Tree of Here, The Sky of Now*, and *Zebra and Other Stories*), but Potok's prolific career ended when he lost his battle with brain cancer and died in his home, in Merion, Pennsylvania, on July 23, 2002. According to obituaries, Potok, working still as a special projects editor for the Jewish Publication Society of America, never missed a single meeting until two weeks before his death, when his failing health finally stopped him in his tracks.

The Story Behind the Story

Chaim Potok's debut novel, *The Chosen*, met with overwhelming critical and popular success upon its release in 1967: it was nominated for the National Book Award, won the Edward Lewis Wallant Prize for Jewish fiction, and spent thirty-eight weeks on the *New York Times'* best-seller list, including a stint at the number one spot. This last fact, of course, indicates how diversified the novel's national readership was from the start, despite the fact that the story focused on two orthodox Jewish families.

Indeed, readers' widespread interest and curiosity about Hasidic Jewish life surprised even the author himself: "I wondered how many Jews would be interested in that tight little world, let alone those who are not Jews, people who haven't the remotest notion of what that world is all about" (Walden 2). The novel's unexpected popularity prompted a scholar, Sheldon Grebstein, to write an entire article on the subject, titled "The Phenomenon of the Really Jewish Best-Seller: Potok's *The Chosen*." In this essay, Grebstein writes, "what would seem an unlikelier best-seller than a first novel by an unknown writer with an unpronounceable name, a novel about orthodox Jews, especially Hasidic Jews, set in the Brooklyn of the early 40s, and a novel whose most stirring action is a schoolboy softball game? ... It is a book totally devoid of such sure-fire elements as violence, sexuality or romantic love" (23). And yet Potok's novel nonetheless beat the odds, selling four hundred thousand hardcover copies and more than three million paperbacks after its release.

Grebstein believes that a number of things contributed to the novel's unlikely success, including its distinctly American sense of optimism; its nostalgia for the time of World War II (when things seemed more black and white than they did in 1967, when Americans faced not only a Cold War but daily controversy surrounding the Vietnam War); and the novel's focus on positive, mature, ever-evolving relationships between two teenaged boys and their fathers. Clearly, this emphasis on family struck a chord at this time, when the generation gap between conservative parents and hippie, counterculture adolescents only seemed to yawn wider and wider. And, significantly, a Methodist fundamentalist from New Orleans first acquired film rights for *The Chosen*, reportedly because he "wanted the world to see that there were American boys who were serious about their studies and about how to relate to their families and the world and that not every American teenager was into drugs and sex and hot rods" (Walden 60).

Many critics and scholars have noted that unlike Phillip Roth, Bernard Malamud, or Saul Bellow—the three giants of Jewish literature—Potok embraces his Jewish identity and writes with great respect and affection for the culture from which he evolved. Rather than trying to escape his Jewish roots (the fictionalized struggle most often portrayed by those writers), Potok grips tightly to them, working to incorporate them into his daily life in the outside world—that is, the secular, humanist society of America.

As Potok himself noted, "I think I have inadvertently stumbled across a cultural dynamic that I didn't quite see clearly myself until sometime toward the end of the writing of *The Chosen*. I think what I am really writing about is culture war" (Walden 4). But while Potok tapped into this timely societal tension—so successfully that *The Chosen* eventually became a film starring Robby Benson and Rod Steiger in 1980—not all the critics embraced him. Some disparaged how Potok slipped from novelist to teacher mode when incorporating relevant aspects of Jewish history into *The Chosen*; some found the dialogue to be stiff and unrealistic; some found the pace to be plodding; and some found Potok's portrait of Hasidic life to be unfair, inaccurate, and pejorative. One dismayed rabbi, Mendel Lipskar, even played on the name of one of Potok's later novels to proclaim staunchly, by way of an article title: "My Name is Not Asher Lev."

But despite these criticisms, which largely came from within the Jewish community, *The Chosen* still remains a coming-of-age classic, often mentioned in the same breath as John Knowles' *A Separate Peace* and Betty Smith's *A Tree Grows in*

Brooklyn. Many teenagers read Potok's novel in school, and its popularity among students appears to stay constant. Teachers appreciate the book's message regarding tolerance, but one of the main reasons for its continued popularity relates to one of the criticisms lobbed against it: it unabashedly teaches readers about Jewish culture and history, a topic few non-Jewish Americans know anything about.

Ironically, though, the book that sparked Potok's desire to write when he was a teenager focused on a Catholic family: Evelyn Waugh's *Brideshead Revisited.* The book was a revelation to Potok, and although the novel seems a strange artistic catalyst for a young man so deeply ensconced in his own family's Hasidic Jewish world, this very contrast was at the heart of Potok's epiphany. In a 1976 interview with Harold Ribalow, Potok explained,

> I lived inside that book with more intensity than I lived inside my own world.... When I closed the book, I was overwhelmed by my relationship to that book. I remember asking myself, "What did he do to me? How do you do this kind of thing with words?" That's where my commitment ... began. (Walden 6)

For Potok, what was most important in Waugh's novel, and what would eventually become most important in his own writing, was the clash between co-existing, dual cultures; for how can you reconcile, in the makeup of your individual identity, your nation's ideology and your ethnic/religious culture in a way that honors both and sacrifices neither? This, quite simply, became the central question of Potok's life and work.

List of Characters

Reuven Malter, who is a teenager at the time of the novel's opening, is an Orthodox Jew and the son of a scholar, and widower, named David Malter. Though he is committed to his religion, Reuven, like his father, tempers his faith with logic, using other areas of study to explore, more comprehensively, the laws found in the Talmud (an idea favored by Potok himself, who converted from Orthodox to Conservative Judaism). By incorporating non-traditional methods, while still remaining an observer of the Commandments, Reuven establishes himself as an assimilated American boy—especially in contrast to Danny Saunders, who exists almost solely within the isolated bubble of his Hasidic community. Reuven is the vehicle through which readers enter into the secret world of the Hasids, and the likable young man's curiosity, judgment, wonder, and admiration not only expose points of anxiety among different sects of Jews, but they also often stand in for the emotions of the secular reader being exposed to this world for the first time.

Danny Saunders, a Hasidic Jew who's Reuven's age, is a brilliant student who feels trapped by an inherited responsibility to his community. Because he is the son of a tzaddik, a figure who acts as a bridge between his people and God, Danny is expected to take his father's place. However, the strict religious and cultural constraints on Danny cause him to pursue his outside interests—specifically Sigmund Freud and the study of psychology—all the more ferociously on his own, in secret. Also, because of his father's perpetual silence, except during Talmud study each Shabbat, Danny has no real outlet for his feelings until he befriends Reuven, with whom he shares an intellectual hunger and a need for friendship.

Reuven's father, **David Malter**, is a teacher at Reuven's yeshiva, or Jewish parochial school. He is a known, well-published scholar, and when news of the Holocaust surfaces at war's end, he becomes a highly vocal activist in the Zionist movement. The time and effort he invests in the cause threaten his already frail heath, but in many ways, David—a character reportedly based on Potok's father-in-law, Max Isaac Mosevitzsky—is an ideal father and teacher. He rationally advises and guides Reuven, with whom he shares a close relationship, while also gently reprimanding him when he makes poor choices.

Danny's father, **Reb Saunders**, is the leader of his Hasidic community, as his father and grandfather had been before him. As tzaddik, he spent years leading his people out of Russia, where they were cruelly persecuted, and into America. But this was not without risk or cost. For although his people were then more free from physical and economic harm in the United States, they were also more exposed to the myriad secular elements on offer in a secular humanist society. In order to keep this from happening, Reb's community isolates itself within one small area of Brooklyn, keeping all the ancient rituals and customs intact. But although the men wear ear locks, black caftans, fringes, and beards, Reb cannot ultimately prevent the curious from entering places like public libraries, where Danny pursues his studies. This presents Reb with an ironic spiritual crisis: what will happen if, after all this effort to preserve the Hasidic community, it dies by virtue of attaining its own longed-for freedoms?

Levi Saunders, Danny's younger brother, is a pale, sickly boy who follows their father into services, his small hand gripping at Reb's caftan from the back. Levi adds an important element to the story, in that he provides a possible escape for Danny— Levi could be tzaddik instead of him—but at the same time, his frailty makes the possibility seem tenuous at best. Also, while Danny is answering his father's questions at services—a practice wherein Reb deliberately plants a mistake and waits for Danny to catch it and articulate it before the other followers—Levi is a figure who never speaks, picks at food (and his nose), and gets rushed to the hospital a number of times. Thus, he functions as a figure of hope, albeit a very shaky one.

Billy Merrit is an eleven-year-old blind boy who shares a hospital room with Reuven (after Danny smacks a baseball into his eye in the book's opening chapter). Billy, who lost both his mother and his sight in a car accident—with his father at the wheel—is sweet, innocent, and upbeat, waiting for an operation that he hopes will give him back his sight. Critics have noted that Billy functions as a catalyst for Reuven's compassion. Like Reuven, who loses sight temporarily in one eye, Billy is in this sad situation through no fault of his own, and his outlook is bleak (no pun intended), making Reuven feel not just sympathy, but gratitude for not being in circumstances quite so dire. Billy helps to give Reuven perspective.

Tony Savo, another resident of the hospital room, is a rough-talking boxer who sasses the nursing staff and listens to radio updates on the war with Reuven. At one point, he tells Reuven that he once considered being a priest, and that religion is a good thing to have as a guide in one's life. In Tony, Reuven sees a man who left the call of his religion, and although he is a nice, good man, he is also one literally beaten by life. Ultimately, Tony loses an eye while in the hospital, again reminding Reuven not only of his good fortune, but of the need for compassion and understanding, particularly in the face of what doesn't seem to make sense.

Summary and Analysis

The Chosen as this novel's title implies has multiple dimensions and potential interpretations. Jews are, according to scripture, God's "chosen people," but because of the Holocaust, and innumerable other horrors committed in the name of anti-semitism throughout history, there often seems to be a sense of irony to this idea, as pointed out by Potok scholar Sanford Sternlicht (Sternlicht 29). Readers must also remember, however, that Jews have nonetheless survived, giving some credence to that moniker. And during the course of Potok's novel, Reuven's father presses the point that according to scripture, a person should choose a friend, as well as allowing him/herself to be chosen by another. This is what happens, with Reuven's father's help, after Danny Saunders and Reuven Malter meet. They choose one another, and what occurs as a consequence composes the core of Potok's novel.

The book begins with the narrator, Reuven Malter, explaining that he lived within five blocks of Danny Saunders for the first fifteen years of his life without knowing of the boy's existence. Danny lived among the Russian Hasidic community, a tight-knit, isolated group that maintained Old World rituals and traditions as much as possible. There are three or four such communities in Reuven's section of Depression-era Brooklyn, each with their own temple, rabbi, and customs. Though they are all Jews, Potok emphasizes the sharp distinctions among the groups immediately, thus indicating the main source of the story's tension and conflict.

Potok describes Williamsburg, Reuven's Brooklyn neighborhood, by way of the disrepair of the sidewalk asphalt; in the summer, it softens, while in the harsh winter, it breaks into potholes. Potok subtly invokes the idea of resistance regarding change—as well as the dangers of exposure—in this passage, forecasting two of the book's main themes.

Most of the neighborhood's houses are three- or four-story brownstones, and they are filled with Jews, Irish, Germans, and Spanish Civil War refugees who had fled before World War II.

Though most of the merchants in the area are non-Jews, Reuven notes that there were a few Orthodox vendors who anxiously waited for holidays so that they could turn their full attention to God, thus emphasizing the central place of religion in their lives.

Reuven explains that all Orthodox Jews send their young sons to a yeshiva, or Jewish parochial school, and although these students' academic burden is already considerable—having to take lessons in Hebrew in the morning and English in the afternoon—the true test of their intellectual capacity still lies in Talmudic study. Danny Saunders attends his father's small yeshiva in Crown Heights, outside Williamsburg, while Reuven attends one in which his own father teaches; this detail is the first indicator that the two father-son pairs will be set in opposition to each other in the novel.

Other yeshivas in Brooklyn look down on Reuven's school because it offers more English courses than is required and because it teaches its lessons in Hebrew instead of Yiddish; both of these elements indicate a level of remove from traditional Jewry that angers and disturbs the Hasids. Most students in Reuven's yeshiva, though, are sons of immigrant couples who want to leave the Old World behind them and who don't want to be part of the isolated, ghetto-like Jewish communities. They believe that assimilation is acceptable, unavoidable, and, ultimately, a positive addition to their identity.

Reuven and Danny Saunders would never meet if not for World War II. Yeshiva faculty members, at the time, want to prove to the larger society that in spite of long hours spent studying, their students are nonetheless as physically fit and able as other American students. To this end, the yeshivas organize athletic teams that compete against each other, and Reuven plays on his school's baseball team.

One Sunday in June, Reuven's team and his gym teacher, Mr. Galanter, wait on the asphalt of his school's play yard. Galanter, a man in his thirties who teaches in a public school as well as Reuven's yeshiva, dresses all in white (a polo shirt, sweater, and pants) except for a black yarmulke. Reuven can tell, by how precariously the skullcap is attached to his teacher's balding head, that he's unaccustomed to wearing it. Significantly, this detail economically connotes Galanter's position; he has so assimilated himself into larger, secular American society that a kipa no longer seems to fit or look natural on his head. Galanter appears, in this way, to be receding from his religion, just as his hair is receding from his head.

Galanter has coached the team for two years and has made such strides that they're now the top team in the league. (The young men did, however, wonder why Galanter wasn't fighting in the war, which ultimately never gets resolved.) Reuven plays second base and sometimes, in key moments, comes in late in a game to throw his patented underhand pitch, which curves downward just as the batter takes his swing. On this particular June afternoon, Reuven's team will play another neighborhood's top team, a group known for their strong hitting and weak fielding.

While warming up, Reuven notes that the rabbis at the yeshivas didn't like the boys playing baseball, seeing it as a step toward assimilation, but among themselves, the students value it highly, believing it demonstrates their patriotism and loyalty to America. Galanter stands at home plate, yelling instructions and bits of encouragement, and Reuven walks from the field to bend down the earpieces of his glasses; he does this so that they stay tightly fastened throughout the game. Scholar Sanford Sternlicht has pointed out the symbolic importance of glasses and eyes in the novel—how events cause characters to "see" differently, and thus understand a different perspective. Regarding characterization, Sternlicht points out that in this opening chapter, Reuven's fiddling with his glasses indicates that he's "a serious student, a reader, but also it foreshadows the accident to his eye that will happen when it is struck by a piece of eyeglass. Glasses are both a way of seeing better and a barrier to the world."

A small boy and sometime-teammate, Davey Cantor, stands at the fence behind home plate and watches Reuven, warning him that their opponents that day are "murderers." Reuven dismisses this, but Davey claims, "They play like it's the first of the Ten Commandments." With this clue, Potok hints that the opposing team will center their determination around their religion and their zealous sense of spiritual superiority and identity. Reuven doesn't take Davey seriously, though, scoffing and jokingly referring to the game as a "holy war." Mr. Galanter calls Reuven to come back to the field, telling him, significantly, "There's a war on, remember?" The statement refers, ostensibly, to World War II, but another, more subtle war is at hand: between assimilated, Americanized Jews and Old World Hasidic Jews.

Reuven hits balls to let others practice fielding when someone calls out that the opposing team is in sight. The fifteen boys approaching wear white sweaters and shirts, black pants, and black kipas. They have closely-shorn heads except for the hair above their ears, which form long corkscrew curls, and sparse facial hair growth. They each wear a traditional undergarment, called a tzitzit, which has a long fringe at each of its four corners, and these cords hang from above their belts and swing against their legs. They are Hasids, the strictest of Orthodox Jews, so they wear their cords outside their clothes to obey the biblical commandment *And ye shall look upon it.* Reuven's team, in contrast, wears jeans, shorts, T-shirts, polo shirts, etc., and while some members wear a tzitzit, none of them wear the cords outside their pants. The only thing the boys on both teams have in common is black yarmulkes, thus noting how tenuous the connection between different sects of Jews in America had already become.

The Orthodox team stands silently behind the home plate fence, and Reuven thinks they don't look threatening, though Davey Cantor nervously kicks at the fence. Mr. Galanter approaches the team, and a young, formally dressed rabbi steps forward. (Reuven wonders why a rabbi is in charge of the team, since it seems a superfluous pursuit that would only take him away from his religious studies.) The rabbi tells Galanter, in Yiddish, that the team's ready to play. Galanter answers in English—another immediate point of difference between the teams—but then the rabbi insists that his team should get to practice on the field while Reuven's team clears off of it. Reluctantly, Galanter grants the opposing team five minutes. The rabbi turns to his team and, in Yiddish, admonishes them to "Remember why and for whom we play," clearly alluding to God. Thus, in spite of Reuven's previous jokes, the game is indeed a "holy war." Significantly, the reason for the boys' play is to prove their strength and agility to mainstream Americans, thus expressing a collective desire on their parts to demonstrate a certain level of assimilation, and yet the degree of assimilation—working in opposition to Old World Jewish traditions, rituals, and beliefs—composes the core of the battle between the two teams. Also, playing baseball, "America's pastime," brings the conflict's irony that much closer to the surface. For here are two groups, fighting over whether their identity as Americans should overwhelm, or even just share in, their identity as Jews, and the battleground for this war is a baseball diamond, home to the most distinctly American sport that exists.

As the game begins and progresses, tensions begin to mount between the two teams. Danny tells Reuven, "I told my team we're going to kill you apikorsim [Yiddish for atheists] this afternoon." Reuven grows angry and realizes the game is no longer merely a game; it is an idealogical, religious, and cultural war. The opposing team, he thinks, has made the game about righteousness vs. sinfulness, but Potok casts a wider net; for in this game, multiple, large-scale battles are being hashed out: Old World vs. New World; Tradition vs. Assimilation; Religious vs. Secular Influences; and Isolation vs. Openness, to name only four. Reuven focuses his rage on Danny, who he comes to hate.

Danny comes up to bat next. Reuven throws a fast ball, but in anticipation of the curve, Danny swings low and hits it right at the mound. Reuven gets his glove up in front of his face, but it deflects off it and smashes into the left lens of his glasses and his forehead. Many critics, of course, have noted that this injury to Reuven's eye demonstrates a deliberate choice by Potok: "The sliver that enters his eye symbolically opens his eyes to the Hasidic world of his friend-to-be" (Sternlicht 44).

Though hurt, Reuven scrambles for the ball, but Danny is safe at first. Galanter calls time and everyone races in to the mound, where Reuven's glasses are in pieces on the asphalt. Reuven's wrist still throbs, he feels a lump forming on his forehead, and there's a sharp pain each time he blinks his left eye. He looks to first, and though he can't see, he imagines Danny grinning. Galanter asks Reuven if he's all right, then shouts for someone to wet a handkerchief with cold water. Reuven isn't sure what the fuss is about; he just busted his glasses, and two other boys on the team could step in and pitch. Galanter walks him off the field and seats him next to the rabbi, though without his glasses, he can't see the game any longer. Galanter soon puts a wet cloth on Reuven's head and asks him if he feels dizzy, which Reuven denies. The rabbi looks at him once, then looks away. The Hasids win, 8–7, and Reuven cries from the pain in his eye. After the game, Galanter takes a look at Reuven's face and runs from the field, calling for a cab.

In **Chapter Two**, Galanter takes Reuven, who feels dizzy and nauseated, to the hospital by cab; the pain in his eye is intense. A nurse instructs them to sit in a waiting room, where they sit next to a middle-aged man with a bloody bandage around one finger. He smokes, despite the sign on the wall that forbids it, and explains that his finger was slammed in a car door by his "kid." Though readers don't learn any further details and the interaction is brief—the man leaves soon when a nurse appears—Potok significantly features a father-child relationship early (Danny has identified Reuven by way of his father, as Davey Cantor identified Danny, too, during the game). Mothers seem invisible or nonexistent in the novel, and in this instance, the child has the power to harm and hurt the father—a small sign of things to come.

A nurse waves Reuven and Galanter into an examination room, where a young doctor looks at Reuven's eye; Galanter excuses himself to call Reuven's father. Reuven asks Galanter to have his father bring his spare pair of glasses, but the doctor explains that Reuven's eye will be bandaged and that he won't be able to wear glasses for a while. Galanter leaves to call, and the doctor examines Reuven's head, wrist, and hand before leaving again, telling Reuven to do his best not to blink.

The doctor returns with an older doctor who says nothing and examines Reuven's eye himself. He tells the first doctor to have Snydman look at Reuven's eye, and the two leave again. After a nurse puts drops in Reuven's eye and leaves, Galanter returns, telling Reuven that his father is on his way. The two doctors come back with a short, friendly, round-faced man. The first doctor introduces the man as Dr. Snydman, who examines Reuven's eye. Snydman tells the other doctors that he'll have to take a closer look upstairs, but that he thinks "it's right on the edge." He tells Reuven that he shouldn't stop balls with his eye, and after a brief, friendly exchange with the patient, he leaves with the other doctors. Reuven asks Galanter for more information, but Galanter doesn't know anything. Two orderlies come in to move Reuven onto a stretcher, but the pain is excruciating for him and he cries out. One of the men apologizes, then they wheel him to the elevator as Galanter follows. In the elevator, the florescent light seems, to Reuven, to be changing color, and he mentions this. The orderlies look at each other, and Galanter mutters, "Jesus." Reuven loses consciousness, noting how everyone crowds around him and the light disappears.

Later, Reuven opens his right eye, hears a nurse ask how he is, and gathers himself after being momentarily disoriented. The nurse asks whether or not he's hungry. He says yes, and she pulls away the curtain that surrounds his bed, flooding him in sunlight. He asks for his father, and she says he'll be there soon and that his dinner is on its way. She leaves, and he carefully looks at his surroundings, settling his gaze on the man on his left, in the next bed. In his thirties, the dark-haired man looks rugged and strong, with a patch over his right eye. Reuven notes that his nose is flat and that there's a scar under his lower lip. He's playing solitaire on his blanket, and he's smiling. He greets Reuven and asks how his head is, using slang like "noggin" and "the old punching bag." He mentions being laid up for a month after getting hit in the head during a boxing match. Reuven doesn't understand much of what the man's saying, so after a moment, he turns his head to the right. There, a ten or eleven year old blond boy lies in bed with his palms behind his head, but he doesn't seem to notice Reuven, who turns away. These two characters in the hospital—though they become Reuven's friends—embody Reuven's temporary immersion into an utterly non-Jewish world. They represent the secular humanist society that makes up most of twentieth-century America, forcing Reuven to face, perhaps for the first time, the dominant culture with which he must negotiate.

Reuven wants to know what day it is, but he doesn't want to disturb the man playing cards, nor the dreamy boy. Soon, though, Reuven hears an orderly come into the ward with dinner. The orderly tells the boy what's on the tray, and the man in the other bed complains that he can't do a ten-rounder on chicken.

A nurse comes to Reuven to say that his father wanted him to know that the hospital is kosher and that he could eat everything. Because he's not supposed to sit up, she raises the bed and gets his skullcap from the nightstand. Reuven places it on his head. The man, Mr. Savo, asks the nurse about the chicken, and after she leaves, he claims that she's "tough as a ring post" though she has a big heart. He tears into his food, and Reuven asks him what day it is. Mr. Savo says it's Monday, and that Reuven had been "out like a light." Reuven introduces himself, resorting to calling himself "Robert" when Savo stumbles over the pronunciation of his true name. The boxer's difficulty here is important because it demonstrates the remove of the Jewish world from dominant American society. Savo isn't refusing to learn the pronunciation or rejecting it because he's anti-semitic; rather, he has no knowledge of Reuven's culture, so to meet him half-way, Reuven chooses to provide him with a similar name that's more familiar, thus laying the foundation for Reuven's tendencies toward reconciling the two cultures.

Savo asks about eating "with a hat on," and whether it's because of Reuven's religion, which he says it is. Savo applauds this and introduces himself, explaining that he's a "prelim man" in prizefighting, largely because of the punch that laid him up for a month. Billy, the blind boy, pipes up, and the two boys introduce themselves. Reuven, who says that Billy can call him "Bobby," explains that he is fifteen years old. Billy asks Reuven to describe himself, and he does: black hair, brown eyes, five feet six inches tall, with "a face like a million others you've seen—you've heard about." Reuven identifies his appearance as almost stereotypically Jewish, though he also realizes that because of Billy's blindness, both literal and figurative (he doesn't "see" Jewish culture), he must adjust his words and perspective. Already, because of the injury, Reuven himself is "seeing" differently.

Billy explains that he's getting an operation so that he might see again. He lost his sight in a car accident with his father, he tells Reuven; once again, notably, we have a father-son relationship in the foreground and no mention of a mother. After dinner, Savo sleeps, and Reuven looks at Billy until he sees a figure rushing down the aisle: his father, David Malter—once again, significantly, no mention is made of Reuven's mother. Critic Edward Abramson wrote, "The stress upon fathers parallels a similar stress in Judaism, where God is King, Judge, and Father.... Thus, the father can be viewed as a fount of wisdom, one who takes upon himself some of the aura of the Godhead" (Abramson 27). However, Sanford Sternlicht found political meanings in the novel's absence of women: "Although Potok does not overtly criticize the patriarchies of the Hasidic family, a reader today cannot but help infer criticism of the marginal role of women in that ultra-religious world, particularly when the reader learns that during worship in the synagogue women are kept behind a curtain of cheesecloth and restricted to a small, rear section of the room" (Sternlicht 42).

David carries a package wrapped in newspaper, and his appearance indicates that he's not faring well: his eyes are red, his face pale, his body thin and worn. David tells Reuven that the hospital called to let him know his son was awake. Sitting on the edge of the bed, Reuven's father sets his package down and tells Reuven that he's been asleep for a day, and that Galanter had called a few times to see how Reuven was doing. Reuven, surprised that there had been an operation, asks about it. His father says that there was glass in Reuven's eye, and that

Dr. Snydman got it out; though David says it was a miracle, he still seems cautious in his enthusiasm. Reuven pleads with his father to tell the truth. Finally, David tells Reuven that the eye is fine and that he can come home in a few days, when the bandages come off, but it will take time to heal.

Just then, a blond man in his thirties comes down the aisle and sits on the edge of Billy's bed, and Reuven realizes that it's the boy's father. Billy sits up, his father kisses his forehead, and they talk quietly. Reuven, resuming the conversation with his own father, says of course it has to heal, but then it dawns on him that the scar tissue might potentially grow over the pupil. Though his father tells him it probably won't happen, he can't guarantee that it won't, and soon, he mentions that Reb Saunders called twice to say that his son is sorry—a message Reuven dismisses sarcastically. Reuven says he hates Danny Saunders, claiming the boy intended to hurt him during the game. He tells his father how Danny's team said that they'd kill the "apikorsim," and that they made the game a war. Mr. Malter, confused, said that Reb Saunders said Danny was sorry, but Reuven again doesn't believe the apology's sincerity. Mr. Malter grows slightly angry, upset with Reuven for making such accusations without foundation, and he insists that Reuven no longer speak that way about Danny. Reuven reluctantly agrees.

David clears away newspaper from the package he brought to reveal a radio, saying that Rome will fall soon and that the European invasion is imminent. He does not want Reuven to forget that there's a world outside the hospital, he claims, and hooks up the radio. This act is significant; as readers soon learn, awareness of, and involvement in, the outside world is something Danny Saunders' father revolts against, for both his family and his community, while David Malter's voiced hope for this goal, regarding his son, demonstrates that although the Malters' aren't wholly assimilated in America, they at least want to take part in the culture and the events of the outside world while maintaining their identity as Jews.

Reuven voices concern about keeping up with his schoolwork—demonstrating the importance of his intellectual life and training to him—but his father tells him he's not allowed to read at all yet. David prepares to leave, saying he has exams to prepare and an article to finish. He stares at Billy and his father, realizing that the boy is blind, and tells Reuven that he has also brought him his tefillin and prayer book. Mr. Malter leaves, and Reuven cries, pondering the possibility of losing sight in his eye permanently. He stares at Billy, who looks up at the ceiling, and Mr. Savo, who's sleeping, and contemplates blindness.

Chapter Three begins as Reuven wakes up hearing voices, and while Billy is sitting up, trying to piece together what's going on, Mr. Savo is gone. A radio is on, broadcasting war news, and soon, Mr. Savo appears at Reuven's bedside. Though the nurses have told Savo to return to his own bed, he first explains to Reuven that the Allies have invaded. The radio announcer reports that the Germans have sunk a Norwegian destroyer. This World War II setting, and discoveries made following the war, are key to the novel; consequential events— namely, the unveiling of the true nature of the Holocaust and the subsequent, controversial quest by Jews to claim Israel— cause changes in the characters' minds and perspectives, thus setting them, at times, in opposition to each other.

After lunch, a six-year-old boy comes into the hospital room bouncing a ball, and Mr. Savo explains to Reuven that the boy's been in the hospital nearly his whole life because of his stomach. The boy stops at Savo's bed, asking him to play catch, but Savo declines because of world events. The boy starts to cry, so Savo agrees to a couple of throws. After only one exchange, though, Mrs. Carpenter storms up the aisle and tells Savo to stop. He's breathing hard and lies back, obeying her. She sends Mickey, the boy, from the ward, and after scolding Savo she soon goes also, leaving him to sleep.

Reuven spots Galanter coming up the aisle. He asks Reuven how he's doing, then talks effusively about the invasion. Reuven says that Billy's uncle is a pilot, and Billy asks Galanter if he's a flyer. The man's face tightens, and Reuven explains that Galanter is his gym teacher. Billy won't relent, though, and he asks why Galanter's not in the war. Galanter struggles to answer, saying he tried to be a soldier but couldn't make it, giving the baseball game, where Jewish boys tried to demonstrate their strength and athletic ability, that much more psychic weight. Galanter, dejected, changes the subject to Reuven's operation, and then he has to leave. When the boys are alone again, Billy expresses sympathy for Galanter, explaining that his own father couldn't fight because Billy's mother had been killed in the same accident that blinded him—the first clearly explained absence of a mother in the novel. Billy then asks that Reuven turn off the radio so he can sleep, and Reuven dozes too, dreaming about his damaged eye. When he wakes, a person is standing near his bed, but in the sunlight, he can't see the face; certainly this description seems to provide the person with extra importance. It's Danny Saunders, who greets Reuven and apologizes for what happened. He wears a dark suit, a black skull cap, earlocks, and fringes below his jacket.

After a moment, Reuven says that he doesn't hate Danny, and Danny takes a seat by Reuven on the bed. Danny asks about the scar tissue, having called David to inquire about Reuven the night before. Reuven, more awake and alert, angrily asks how it feels to blind someone. Danny's face goes expressionless, and the two argue: Danny says there's nothing more he can say, and Reuven condemns him and bids him leave. He does, apologizing once more, and Reuven is left shaking, frightened by his own anger. Savo asks about Danny, and Reuven explains that the boy's responsible for his eye injury. Reuven says he wants to sleep, and while coming to regret his behavior, he watches Savo play solitaire. It's worth noting that while Billy and Reuven receive visitors, no one comes to see Savo, and he always plays solitaire. He is truly alone in the world: a gentile without a family or a community.

That evening, David Malter comes to visit, and Reuven explains what happened. Angry, Mr. Malter admonishes Reuven, then quickly apologizes for scolding him. He reiterates, though, that Reuven must learn to be patient and listen, then changes the subject, wanting to discuss the war. He leaves, and soon Billy's father comes. He talks to Reuven and tells him that after Billy's surgery, they'd like to have Reuven over to their home, so Billy can see him. Reuven agrees, then lies back in bed, depressed.

The following morning Danny arrives for another visit. Though more cautious, he sits on Reuven's bed, and Reuven apologizes. Danny tells him that he's been thinking about the game and that he doesn't understand why he wanted to kill Reuven. Reuven offers that it might have just been the heat of competition, but Danny insists it's more than that. Danny says that his team had played other good squads and had even lost before, but Reuven had really gotten under his skin, and he can't figure out why.

Reuven wonders, in this moment, at the strangeness of the situation—how quickly a friendship seemed to be developing from animosity. He's surprised by how clearly this Hasid can converse in English; most Hasids had only spoke to him before in Yiddish. Even the two boys' names, however, seem in opposition to their lives and communities; Reuven, living in a more permissive cultural hodgepodge of American Jewishness, has a name that's difficult for non-Jews to pronounce, while Danny Saunders, who lives in the utterly strict Hasid world, has a recognizable, seemingly assimilated name that's easy for non-Jews to say.

Both boys praise the other's softball skill, and Reuven asks how Danny learned to hit, saying, "I thought you people always studied Talmud." Danny explains that he worked out a deal with his father, wherein after four pages of Talmud study a day, his time was his own. Reuven, who considers one page of Talmud a day to be strenuous, wonders at this, and Danny explains that only he has to work at this pace, because of his father. Danny asks what page Reuven is studying now, and upon hearing the answer, Danny mechanically recites the page from memory, including commentaries and legal decisions. Danny explains to Reuven that he's got a photographic memory, and Reuven asks if Danny will be a rabbi. He answers yes, and that he will take his father's place. Reuven says he might also be a rabbi, and Danny wonders at this, stating that he could be so many other things. This surprises Reuven, and

Danny says that if he had a choice, he'd like to pursue psychology. Once again, Danny doesn't seem to fit Reuven's pre-conceived notion, but this is true of the novel's readers as well. Danny, the Jew of Old World customs, culture, and beliefs, speaks English well and longs to study psychology, an utterly secular field, while Reuven, who has the choice to pursue anything, chooses the study of the religion that's not the center of his life but merely a part.

Reuven tells Danny that if he doesn't become a rabbi, he'd teach math, but he feels as though he'd be more useful to people as a rabbi. He asks Danny about the rabbi who sat on the bench reading, and Danny explains that the man's a teacher at his yeshiva, sent along to make sure the boys don't mix too much with the "apikorsim." Danny then says that the only way he could convince his father to field a team from the yeshiva was to convince him that they "had a duty to beat you apikorsim at what you were best at." Reuven asks what would happen if they had lost, and Danny darkly and vaguely alludes to his father's strict ways, leading Reuven to the conclusion that Danny's team truly *had* to beat Reuven's.

Reuven asks about what the rabbi was reading, thinking it was something of Reb Saunders', but Danny explains that his father doesn't write. Reb feels that words distort the heart's contents, and indeed, only talks to Danny when they study Talmud together. With just this piece of information, readers already get a sense of how different Danny's relationship with Reb is from Reuven's relationship with David. Readers witnessed already how openly, lovingly, and encouragingly the Malters speak to each other, while here we learn that Danny and Reb speak not at all, other than Talmud study.

Absorbed by his troubling admission, Danny distractedly bids Reuven goodbye, saying that he'll be back to visit the next day, and he leaves.

A few minutes later, at the opening of **Chapter Four**, David Malter comes in, looking pale and ill. He tells Reuven that Dr. Snydman will see him on Friday, and then he can come home, but he still can't read for another ten days. Reuven is just thrilled by the idea of going home.

Reuven tells Mr. Malter of Danny's visit and their conversation. David rather vehemently insists that Reuven make Danny his friend, and then inquires about Billy, who sleeps in the next bed. Reuven explains that the accident that blinded the boy also killed his mother, stirring pity in David. He leaves then, telling Reuven he'll be back the next day.

After David leaves, Mr. Savo asks about him, and Reuven tells him he's a teacher. Savo also asks about Danny and warns Reuven not to trust him completely. Because of Danny's Orthodox dress, Savo views him as a fanatic and tells Reuven to stay watchful. (Like Potok, it seems, Savo believes religious fanaticism to be ultimately destructive.)

In the night, Reuven wakes, disoriented, and sees that the curtain around Savo's bed has been drawn. He hears people moving around, and a tense nurse tells him to go back to sleep, so he does. In the morning, though, the curtain is still drawn around Savo's bed, and Mrs. Carpenter is moving down the aisle. While eating breakfast, Reuven sees Dr. Snydman and Mrs. Carpenter approach and go through Savo's curtains. All day the curtain stays drawn, and Reuven's so worried he can hardly eat, but Danny's approach down the aisle finally lifts his spirits. After going out into the hall so as not to disturb Savo, the boys settle on a bench and talk about how they were both born at this hospital. Danny comments, while watching the doctors and nurses rush by, that people look like ants, and that he felt sometimes that that's all they were (indicating Danny's philosophical frame of mind). He's told his father this, but he got no response until days later, when Reb Saunders told him that a Jew's mission is to obey God. Again, this sets Danny and Reb in contrast to Reuven and David, who speak so openly that it's hard to imagine a response that's not immediate. Reuven asks if Danny believes Reb's conclusion, and Danny says yes, though he's not sure what God wants. Though distant, Danny continues, explaining that he reads seven or eight books a week in addition to his schoolwork, including books by Darwin and Huxley (secular thinkers whose writings were forbidden among the Hasids). Danny reads in the library secretly, because his father is strict about what he reads. Currently, he's reading

Hemingway's *A Farewell to Arms*. He gets bored with the Talmud, he says, and there's a man at the library who keeps suggesting books for Danny.

Reuven confesses that Danny confuses him; that he doesn't sound like a Hasid, and that he talks as if he didn't believe in God. Danny doesn't respond—ironically making him seem far more akin to the "apikorsim" than Reuven—and Reuven asks if Danny's really planning to take his father's place as a rabbi. He says yes, and that he believes in God, though Reuven remains skeptical. Danny explains again that he has no choice, and that the up side is that when he's a rabbi, he'll be able to read what he wants and no one will question him. Though he doesn't want to be a rabbi, he (significantly the "chosen" successor) feels the weight of generations before him and the obligation to serve his community. Danny points out the irony between them: Danny doesn't want to be a rabbi but has no choice, and Reuven could be anything but wants to be a rabbi.

Danny asks Reuven about his interest in math; Reuven says he's primarily interested in mathematical logic, and that he pursues its study on his own—though he only reads three or four books each week. In these exchanges, readers again see how vital and important intellectual exercise is to these young characters: they are willing to dedicate all their leisure time to extra-academic pursuits. Reuven spots his father coming from the elevator, and Danny's expression changes from curiosity to nervous wonder. Reuven introduces his friend to his father, and the two stare at each other until David finally remarks that Danny must play ball as well as he reads books; David is the man at the library who has suggested books for Danny. David explains how he sat at the table one day and Danny approached him, asking for recommendations; after David gave him one, he came back two hours later, asking for more. Soon, the two discussed the books Danny read, though Danny demurs when asked his name, so David later finds out who the boy is from the librarian.

In the hospital, Danny thanks David for his suggestions and says he will keep coming to the library. He must leave, but first he tells Reuven that he'll come see him at home on Saturday.

Danny leaves, and Reuven and his father exchange a quiet few words, watching Billy's sad father walk toward the elevators. Reuven soon walks David to the elevator and turns back to the eye ward, where now not only is Savo's curtain drawn, but also Billy's. Reuven goes to the nurses' station to inquire, but they insist that Billy's just asleep and that Reuven should sleep also.

The next morning, Savo greets him. His curtain has been pulled back, and there's a bandage where his eye patch used to be. Reuven's happy to see him, but when Reuven looks to Billy's bed, Savo explains that the boy left for surgery two hours before. Savo then lies back to sleep, and Reuven prays for Billy. Soon, though, Reuven's in an examination room, and Dr. Snydman takes the boy's bandage off. After adjusting to the light in the room, feeling the cold on his eye, Reuven realizes that he can see. Dr. Snydman says Reuven can go home, but he wants to see him in ten days. Snydman says that he can't be sure, but he thinks Reuven will be all right.

When leaving with Mrs. Carpenter, Reuven asks about Billy, and the nurse evasively says that they always hope for the best. Reuven tells Savo the news, and he's excited for him. Getting dressed in the clothes he last wore at the ball game, Reuven waits nervously for his father, who finally appears. Reuven says goodbye to Savo and learns that he lost his eye. He hadn't said anything before because he didn't want to scare Billy; Reuven expresses sympathy for Savo, and he and his father leave the hospital.

Though Savo only appears briefly in the novel, he represents secular American society. He's a good person, albeit wholly different from Reuven in terms of values, experience, and perspective, and this is one thing Reuven "sees" by virtue of his accident. Gentiles aren't bad, terrifying people; instead, they are by and large decent, hard-working, cheerful, lonely, tough, and, most pitiably, spiritually adrift. Potok scholar Edward A. Abramson took this point further, arguing that Savo's presence raises the issue of faith in the novel, particularly in contrast to violence; Savo himself once wanted to be a priest, but now he's a boxer—paid to commit and receive violence—and he complains bitterly about his manager not having faith. Add to this the radio broadcasts about the violence in Europe, Abramson says, and readers get a sense of "Potok's feeling that violence implies a lack of faith both in mankind and in something greater than man" (Abramson 16).

Billy, on the other hand, evokes compassion and a grounded sense of perspective in Reuven. Billy's circumstances are more tragic than Reuven's, and therefore, Reuven "sees" that his situation could be far worse, thus making him a more understanding, sympathetic human being.

Chapter Five begins with Reuven and his father riding home in the cab and Reuven's father gives him his other pair of glasses. Though Reuven can't read until the doctor says it's OK, everything pops into focus when he puts on his glasses. He and his father live on the first floor of a three story brownstone, and as they enter the apartment, Reuven smells chicken soup. Manya, the Russian housekeeper, runs from the kitchen to greet him.

Reuven and his father eat a lunch feast, prepared by Manya, and then Mr. Malter goes to his study to work on an article. Reuven walks through the apartment, overwhelmed by how new everything now appears to him, emphasizing again how much his perspective has shifted in this short time. His room, a narrow space, has *New York Times* war maps on the wall near his bed, as well as torn out magazine photos of Albert Einstein and Franklin Delano Roosevelt. The door to his father's study, where he hears a typewriter tapping, stands near the head of his bed, and he must pass through the study to reach the living room. He enters the study quietly. The room is the same size as his room, though there are no windows, and the walls are covered floor-to-ceiling with bookcases. Mr. Malter sits at his desk typing, wearing his black skull cap and surrounded by scattered papers. He frowns, not liking to be disturbed, and Reuven moves through the study to the living room. There, Reuven stood at the windows a long time, watching children play in the street. Soon, he goes through his father's bedroom to reach the back porch, where he sits and contemplates the change in himself since the game. He feels like a completely different person, though the surroundings are familiar. He thinks about Danny visiting him the next day, pondering this new presence in his life.

The chapter's function, primarily, is to establish the warm environment that is the Malters' home. Though the absence of Reuven's mother is still not explained or noted, Manya temporarily, nominally fills that domestic void, and the closeness of the apartment's rooms indicates the closeness of the father and son. Lastly, Reuven's observation of the children playing underlines that he is no longer truly a part of the world of children.

After the Shabbat meal that night, when Manya had cleaned and left, Reuven and his father linger at the kitchen table (**Chapter Six**). David says that in order to explain Danny's circumstances, he must mine facts from Jewish history, preparing Reuven for a long tale—the birth of the Hasidic movement.

After David explaines the history of Hasids, he says that Danny's father, Reb Saunders, is a great scholar and tzaddik who believes that soul is more important than mind, and that Danny will inherit his father's position. David then says that Reuven should keep Danny in mind as he hears the next story, one of a Polish boy in the second half of the seventeenth century. The boy, Solomon, had been a genius, though he later changed his Polish name to Maimon. As a boy, Talmudic study could not satisfy his thirst for knowledge. He wanted to learn things from the world outside his community, but he could not, since secular books were forbidden. At age twenty-five, however, he left his wife and child to escape to Berlin, where he read the work of philosophers, found a set of intellectual peers, and wrote his own philosophical tracts. He couldn't settle down, though, and traveled from place to place until he died at forty-seven.

Danny's mind is like Solomon Maimon's, Malter says, and Danny lives in free America, making it easy for him to venture into forbidden areas of knowledge. He's an intellectual phenomenon, according to David, but Danny doesn't have a person in the world to whom he can talk. The baseball incident binds him and Reuven, and Danny already trusts him, or else he wouldn't have told him about the library visits. David wants the two to be friends, he says in conclusion.

Reuven voices how strange it is that everything in his life has shifted because of a baseball game, and he explains to his father how, when he came home from the hospital, everything seemed new. David smiles and says that he wishes Reuven's mother were alive to see him, when David is overcome with emotion. Reuven goes to bed, leaving his father at the kitchen table.

This last passage, of course, is the first mention of Reuven's mother's death, but it is a passing detail more than a motive for action or emotion. Reuven and David seem a wholly complete family unit.

Primarily, this chapter fills in the historical context of the story. By knowing the history of the Hasids, readers get a clearer, stronger sense of Danny's burden as the son of a tzaddik. Many critics, though, thought Potok slipped into the role of pedantic lecturer in these passages, bogging down the narrative's momentum; Sternlicht, citing "Potok's role as teacher/writer," defended the inclusion of a lecture on Jewish history in the novel, though, noting that "the serious reader should slow down and absorb the lessons. There is much to be learned from Chaim Potok" (Sternlicht 44). Significantly, regardless of the history's placement or emphasis in the novel, the conflict between religious tradition and modern secular knowledge is highlighted, thus raising the stakes for Danny, the true focus of the novel.

The next day (**Chapter Seven**), Reuven goes with his father to synagogue—a converted grocery store—where other teachers and students from their yeshiva worship. Afterward, when Reuven and his father have lunch, David says that Reuven can return to school and listen, but he is still forbidden to read. Reuven later sits out on the porch and falls into a "half-sleep that refreshes but does not shut off the world completely." Even while unconscious, Potok seems to indicate, Reuven is more open to the outside world than the Hasids.

While in this haze, Reuven opens his eyes to find Danny before him. He tells Reuven that it's after five o'clock and suggests that they go to his father's shul, since Reb wants to meet Reuven. Reuven cleans up and they head out. Walking along the street, Reuven asks Danny why his father wants to meet him. Not surprisingly, Danny tells him that Reb Saunders has to approve of all his son's friends, especially those outside their Hasid community.

Danny asks Reuven about brothers and sisters, but Reuven explains that his mother died soon after his birth. Danny has a fourteen-year-old sister and an eight-year-old brother, but he's the oldest at sixteen, the same age as Reuven. (This information may seem jarring to readers at first; previous to this—particularly at the baseball game—the two boys seem younger, lacking sexual interest or curiosity, and many scholars have long criticized the corny clunkiness of much of their dialogue.) The two were born only two days apart, and Reuven remarks on how they could live so close for so long without knowing each other, echoing the book's opening. Danny says that it's not surprising, since his father doesn't like his followers to mix with outsiders, and Reuven says that Danny's father sounds like a tyrant. Danny explains that Reb is strong-willed, and although Reb almost never talks to Danny outside of Talmud study, Danny made a point to tell Reb about Reuven. This was the only personal interaction he had had with him, apart from convincing him about the baseball team. Though Reb's silence bothers Danny, he still admires his father greatly.

Reuven asks if Danny's brother will be a rabbi, and Danny becomes angry. He soon goes back to discussing Reb, who he admires for leading his community from Russia to America after World War I. Reuven's impressed, and Danny explains further. Reb had been the second son in his family, but the first son vanished under mysterious circumstances while studying in Odessa; this being true, the position of rabbi fell to Reb at age seventeen, a tale which yields two important details: Reb himself was a second son called to lead, and Reb's own brother, like Danny, seems to have been tempted from the insular world of the Hasids. Following Reb's father's death, Reb became tzaddik at age twenty-one, and after the First World War, his wife, newborn son, and toddler daughter were shot by a bandit gang of Cossacks. Reb himself had a bullet lodged in his chest and a saber wound in his pelvis, and the Cossacks left him for dead. But soon the synagogue's custodian, a Russian peasant, found Reb and moved him to his hut, where the peasant tended to Reb's wounds.

The temple had been destroyed by fire, and of the more than one hundred Jewish families in the community, only forty-three remained. One such family, upon learning of Reb's survival, took him into their home to finish nursing him back to health. Russia, meanwhile, pulled out of the war, but chaos within its borders proved just as lethal. Reb's village was raided by Cassocks four times, but each time, sympathetic Russian peasants warned the Jews, and the residents scattered among the woods or in huts. Soon, Reb announced to his people that they were through with Russia, and that they would go to America.

After five months of bribing and bargaining their way across countries, they finally landed at Ellis Island. They settled in the Williamsburg section of Brooklyn, where three years later, Reb re-married; his first son from this marriage, Danny, was born two days before the stock market crash. This harrowing, tragic backstory for Reb sets up readers to have some sympathy and understanding for his perspective. He has suffered greatly for his faith and his people, so his actions don't stem from malevolence; rather, he wishes to properly prepare Danny to assume his post as tzaddik.

Reuven wonders aloud at Reb's power, asking how people could follow one man so blindly. Danny explains that Reb is the bridge between his people and God, and Reuven remarks that this sounds like Catholicism. The boys turn a corner and though quite similar to Reuven's street, Danny's block lacks flowers, and the brownstones are generally older and less carefully maintained. Trash blew around on the street, and women in long sleeves and kerchiefs, often with children in their arms or pregnant, sat on steps and spoke Yiddish. Reuven, nervous and feeling displaced, concentrates on the sound of Danny's metal-capped shoes as they climb the steps of a brownstone and enter a synagogue, which is the size of the modest apartment he shares with his father.

Men mill around, and then Dov Shlomovitz enters, staring coldly at Reuven. He takes a seat, and Reuven tells Danny, in a low voice, that he feels like a cowboy surrounded by Indians; though they are all Jews, the distinctions between the groups are sharp. Reuven voices wonder at the men's deference to Danny outside, and Danny explains that as heir to his father's position, Danny deserves the utmost respect from all within the community. The boys sit down as the men file into the temple.

Two elders approach Danny to settle a disagreement about a Talmud passage's interpretation. Danny identifies and repeats, word for word, the passage and dispenses his interpretation of it, quoting commentators along the way. He tells them that they are both right, in a way, and the men smile and leave. Danny admits to Reuven, though, that the passage is baffling, and that Reuven's father David would probably say that the text is wrong. (This forecasts Reuven's own struggle, and conclusions, regarding a difficult passage later, when he is in college.) Danny has smuggled David's articles from his father's desk to read, so he knows Reuven's father's methods and ideas.

Reuven opens the old, yellowed prayer book before him, so different from the new one he had used at his own temple that morning; this emphasizes again, albeit subtly, that one community lives in the past while the other embraces the present. The noise in the room ceases, and a tall man in a black satin caftan and a fur-trimmed black hat makes his way up the aisle, while a young boy trails behind him. The men bow, and some lean out to touch him. He looks like Danny, though his eyes and hair are much darker, and the boy—who holds onto Reb's caftan with one hand—is a "delicate miniature" of the man, dressed in the same clothes: Danny's brother, Levi.

Reb approaches Reuven and Danny, and they stand. Danny introduces Reuven in Yiddish, and Reuven knows that Reb is staring at his injured eye. Reb asks Reuven, almost accusingly, if he's the son of David Malter, and Reuven nods. He knows he should answer in Yiddish, but his grasp of the language is poor, so he responds in English. Reb asks about his eye, and Reuven says that it's fine, realizing that everyone is watching and listening. Soon, Reb steps up to a podium, his back to the congregation. The boys sit, and the service gets underway.

The meeting ends with the Kaddish, the prayer for the dead. Reb heads back up the aisle again with the boy in tow, and Danny nudges Reuven to rise and follow Reb. The four sit at a table, and the other men, after singing and clapping, assemble at tables of their own. Reb stands, washes his hands, and says a blessing over the bread, followed by Danny and Reuven. As Reb finishes his food, someone clears his plate away, and Danny fills another plate for him. Reuven isn't hungry and picks at his food, as does Danny's young brother, who Reuven notes is dark-featured like Reb, but pale, skinny, and frail-looking.

No words are spoken during the meal, but Reuven can feel Reb's eyes on him. The meal ends in song, which Reuven joins in singing. Reb smiles, but soon he stands, and after a long silence he speaks, reciting a passage that states that if people follow God's will, He will follow their will, and vice versa. The contradiction, Reb explains, is that people are powerless, so why should God do their will?

According to Reb Saunders, God is inside the man who does His will, thus raising that man from his lowly, powerless status as a human. But doing God's will is not simple, Reb says. Someone who gets distracted from his study by the outside world may forfeit his life, according to scripture; at this, Danny quickly looks at his father, then lowers his eyes. His body goes limp, he fights a smile, and he sighs; this body language, astutely described by Potok, indicates that Danny and Reb perpetually have this unspoken tension between them about this issue. Reb asks whose task it is to study the Torah. Not the world's, he argues—saying that the world is Hitler and the Cossacks, among other villains, thus demonstrating the narrow view Reb has of the outside world—but rather the Jew's.

Reb argues that the Hasids' isolated community is the pure way to God, and then he breaks down the words "this world" by way of numerology, or "gematriya." Reuven explains that each Hebrew letter is also a number, such that every Hebrew word has a numerical value, which may then be interpreted in some way. Reb pursues this exercise with several different words and phrases, gleaning spiritual messages from numerical equations. Near the speech's end—when Reb emphasizes that when we study the Torah, God listens and fulfills our wishes— he stares pointedly at Danny. Reuven smiles but confesses to readers that he doesn't agree with Reb's pessimism. Einstein, Roosevelt, and the soldiers fighting Hitler are part of the outside world, too, he argues, just as much as the villains Reb named.

Everyone stares at Danny, and Reb sits and crosses his arms over his chest. With some prodding, Danny finally speaks, correcting his father on the name of one of rabbis he referenced. The crowd murmurs approval, and Reb nods and asks Danny if there were other mistakes. Danny says no. Reuven realizes that what he's witnessing is a more tense, more public version of a Shabbat afternoon ritual, in which the learned father quizzes his son on what he has learned that previous week, emphasizing the priority that's placed on learning in Jewish families. Danny, however, seems involved in more of a contest than a quiz, and what he's expected to know isn't limited to an isolated part of the Talmud, but rather from the whole. Reb asks Danny more questions, the answers to which require memorization of passages as well as conflicting commentaries. Danny supplies all answers without strain, and Reuven sits in wonder, watching Reb and Danny.

In a book review of *The Chosen*, Judah Stampfer complained that Reb Saunders' deliberate mistakes—among several other elements of Potok's portrayal of Hasids—rang false: "Such a gesture no Hasidic rebbe would ever do before his congregation. A holy man, a voice of God's truth, does not engage in such devious gestures in public. It rings tricky, and goes against the whole grain of the institution" (Stampfer 495). Despite such claims about Potok's faulty portrait of Hasids, however, Edward A. Abramson wrote, "Potok's descriptions of Hasidic rigidity and dislike of outsiders seems convincing, even if certain details may not be completely accurate" (Abramson 14).

In the temple, the quiz ends, but Reb presses Danny on

whether or not anything else in the service needed correction. Danny tenses up and says no, but Reb keeps asking, admonishing Danny for listening only until he heard the mistake. Reb shifts his gaze to Reuven, sighs and shakes his head and says that his son isn't a mathematician, but Reuven is. Reb asks Reuven if he noticed anything wrong. After initially freezing up, Reuven says that not all of the gematriya were good: one of the words he used comes to five hundred and three, not five hundred and thirteen. Reb smiles broadly, and Danny and Reuven relax, realizing that Reuven's passed a kind of test.

After the evening service, the men all exit the room, leaving Reuven alone with Danny, Reb, and Levi. Reb sighs and shakes his head again, saying that he is glad Danny and Reuven are friends. He's not surprised that Reuven is bright, since he is David Malter's son, and though he's worried because of the scientific method-based articles that David Malter writes, he takes comfort in the fact that Reuven's father lives by the Commandments. This comment throws the two fathers into direct contrast, wherein rigid, Old World Reb faces off against David, who rationally brings together the best elements of the religious and secular worlds to achieve an advantageous balance in his life and work.

Reb is glad Danny has friends, because he, himself, has many responsibilities and cannot always talk to his son. (Already it's clear that Reuven is a conduit through which Reb speaks to Danny.) Reb tells Reuven that it will not be easy to be a good friend, then turns to leave, his youngest son trailing behind. Reb and Danny had said nothing to each other all day, Reuven realizes, outside of the Talmud quiz.

Danny walks Reuven home, noting that Reuven must see Reb as a tyrant. Reuven says that Reb seems a tyrant one moment, kind the next. Reuven asks about the quizzing, which Danny confirms happens every week. It's a family tradition, and Reb makes mistakes he knows Danny can catch, as if playing a game; thus, here is another arena wherein the father and son understand one another, yet they don't speak of it. The gematriya error, Danny says, was clearly for Reuven, but it also provided Reb with an opportunity to catch Danny not listening, which he admits he wasn't. He argues, though, that even if he had been listening, he wouldn't have caught it, since his photographic memory does him no good in math. Reuven asks what happens if Danny misses the mistake, and though it's been years since he has, Danny says Reb would make a joke and re-engage in a Talmud discussion. The congregants are proud of Reb and Danny and love to hear these exchanges, he explains.

Reuven asks if Reb always does gematriya, and Danny says no. Although it's popular, and the men hope for it, Reb seldom does it. He used to be better at it, but he's been worried about Levi lately. Danny explains that although he doesn't know exactly what ails his brother, it has something to do with his blood, and he's had trouble for years. Danny insists that his brother will be fine, such that Reuven concludes he must love his brother very much, though he didn't see them exchange a word.

Danny says the quizzes will stop once he's studying with Rav Gershenson at Hirsch College. Reuven's excited by this news. He and his father always assumed that that's where he would pursue further education beyond high school, and he tells Danny. Danny's pleased and says he plans to study psychology. When they reach Reuven's synagogue, Danny invites Reuven to come to the library the next afternoon. Though he can't read yet, he says he'll come anyway, and Danny leaves.

Reuven tells his father everything he witnessed that day (again in contrast to Danny and Reb); David grimaces upon hearing about the gematriya, which, Reuven explains, his father considers "nonsense numerology." Reuven tells of catching the mistake, what Reb said after the service, and his and Danny's discussion about college on the way home. David appears pleased. Reuven protests, though, that he thought the quiz cruel and terrible. His father explains that it's not terrible to Danny, or Reb, or the men in that room, but rather an old tradition that is sometimes adopted in the world of academics. David argues that the congregants must see that their future leader has a strong grasp on these things, and though it might seem cruel, learning must be shared or it's a waste. David does remark, however, that the "mistake" ritual is an innovation of Reb Saunders', and that he doesn't like it.

Reuven doesn't know what to make of Reb. David says he's a great man, and that it's hard to be a great leader because of all the responsibility. In David's opinion, it's a shame that Reb focuses solely on the Talmud and won't, as a result, contribute to the larger world. Danny, too, will have to follow the same path, which David regrets. After a quiet moment, David shifts his focus back to Reuven, telling him he's proud of how his son handled himself, and that he's glad Reuven and Danny will be friends. Reuven goes to bed, leaving his father sitting at the kitchen table.

In this chapter, for the first time, readers can directly contrast the two father-son relationships. Critic Sam Bluefarb observed,

> The Saunderses seem to have an excess of head in their makeup; but the Malters have heart *and* head: they are in balance....
>
> Reuven's studies are "brain" disciplines—logic, mathematics, philosophy—yet it is he who finally turns out to have more "heart" than the brilliant son of a Hasid. Danny, on the other hand, having been raised in the tradition of the Ba'al Shem, should have been a "heart-and-joy specialist." Yet it is he who is all brain. (407)

In **Chapter Eight**, Reuven returns to school to find himself a hero, by way of his baseball performance and injury; though only a week has passed, everything looks different to him now. Sidney Goldberg and Davey Cantor approach him at recess to talk about the game, but this strikes Reuven as silly now.

After school, Reuven goes to the public library to meet Danny. A quote from Keats about truth and beauty is engraved in stone above the entrance, and trees, a lawn, and flowers compose the area in front of the library. Upon entering, Reuven finds a mural of great thinkers, which includes both religious figures, like Jesus and Mohammed, with giants of science, like Galileo, Copernicus, Newton, and Einstein. On the opposite wall, a mural of great writers spans the space. All these images of the library represent that which Danny is not allowed—officially—to notice or explore. His father, and Hasids in general, think that to remain pure and be a bridge to God, one must refuse outside temptations and stay focused on the Talmud, but it is precisely these secular studies and ideas that fascinate Danny. Also, ironically, the beauty of nature outside the library hearkens back to the story of Israel, the original founder of the Hasids, who chose to venture into the woods instead of sitting in a classroom.

Reuven notes that in the mural, Homer's eyes seem to have no pupils, and he speculates that the painter had tried to communicate his blindness in this way; Reuven's startled that he hadn't noticed this before. In this passage, Potok subtly underlines how Reuven himself had been blind, in a way, previous to his injury. After having almost lost his sight, his vision, and powers of perception, seem more powerful and focused than before.

Reuven finds Danny hunched over a book in a corner on the third floor. Few people settled there, among the scholarly journals, and Reuven notes it's the floor with which he's least familiar. He'd been there once to look up an article on logic, and once to meet his father, but that had been it. Reuven observes how Danny reads quickly, down the center of each page. Reuven sits at a nearby table so as not to disturb Danny, but he feels frustrated at being surrounded by books he can't read. Instead, he works through symbolic logic problems with his eyes closed. Danny accuses him then of always sleeping, and Reuven opens his eyes and says he was doing an indirect proof. Danny beckons Reuven to sit near him and listen to something from a book titled *History of the Jews*. Dov Baer, a follower of the Besht (i.e., a Hasid), invented the idea of the tzaddik, Danny explains, then he reads a passage that states that many tzaddiks profited from the system, because their followers were required to bring them expensive gifts and attend to their wants and needs. The book's author, Graetz, compares these leaders with the priests of Baal, calling them vulgar and disgusting, which disturbs Danny greatly. Regarding Dov Baer, the book says that he made vulgar jokes and encouraged his followers to drink so they would pray more fervently. When one opponent of Hasidism died, the men danced on his grave, celebrating with shouts and alcohol. Danny knows nothing of this and asks Reuven if anyone at shul the day before looked drunk. Reuven says no.

Danny's father doesn't resemble what's described in the book at all; he worries about his people to a fault, Danny notes. Reuven suggests that Graetz is commenting on the Hasidim of his own time, but this is no comfort to Danny, who hates how this image of his community, and thus himself, has been cast. The inclusion of this text in Potok's novel provides a sense of the hostility many Jews have historically felt toward Hasids, as well as the exaggerated, propagandistic nature of such partisan claims. Though Potok's own biased criticisms regarding Hasidism reveal themselves subtly throughout the novel, he nonetheless strives to maintain a degree of objectivity and be fair.

Reuven asks if David recommended the book, and Danny said he simply suggested that Danny read about Jewish history and learn about his own people. Reuven urges Danny to talk with David about it, underlining the irony that Danny can speak to Reuven's father, but not his own. Danny starts to explain how a psychology book he'd read the previous week said "the most mysterious thing in the universe to man is man himself." This leads Danny to the idea of the subconscious, which, he says, dominates everyone's life. He tells Reuven about how the subconscious constructs dreams, though the messages are often encoded in symbols. Psychoanalysis, he says, helps unlock the subconscious, and he's learning German so that he may read Freud's work in its original form. Learning German, however, as critic Sternlicht observed, "the language then of the mortal enemies of the Jews, is an unconscious double act of aggressive rebellion and revenge against [Danny's] father that Reuven senses but Danny disavows" (47).

Indeed, Reuven goes cold at the notion of Danny learning and speaking German, but Danny defends himself, saying that just because Hitler speaks the language doesn't mean it's corrupt. Danny's memorized a German grammar book already, and he starts rattling off words to demonstrate how precise the language is. He notes how close its ties are to Yiddish, since the German Jews who came into Poland brought this "middle German" language with them.

Reuven explains to readers that his discomfort doesn't stem from Hitler, but rather from his father's tale of Maimon, and how closely Danny seems to be following the same path. Soon, though, the two start talking about Danny's brother, who saw a doctor earlier that day. He's fine, according to Danny, but he must avoid strenuous exercise and studying. Reb was sad at the news, and Danny's brother has to take three pills a day, perhaps for the rest of his life.

The two decide to leave, but as they go down the stairs, Danny stops at each floor and looks around, indicating that he is afraid of being caught. He puts the Graetz book back on its shelf, and the two take a trolley car home.

Reuven, at dinner, tells his father about Danny's latest pursuit, explaining that he wants to read Freud. David shakes his head and mutters that it will be impossible to stop Danny. Reuven, though, asks if Graetz was accurate in his portrayal of the Hasidim. David says the author was biased and his sources inaccurate, noting that there was enough to dislike about Hasidism without blowing their faults out of proportion—something Potok himself seems to want to emphasize.

Later in the week, Reuven meets Danny in the library again, but Danny isn't cheered by the news of David's critique of Graetz; Danny has already read another book that also painted an awful picture of the tzaddikim.

That night, Reuven's father voices ethical qualms about recommending books to Danny behind his father's back. He reasons, however, that Danny would read secular works regardless, and by way of David's intervention, Danny's receiving guidance from an adult. Reuven says that Danny's already reading things on his own, anyway; David certainly never suggested that Danny read Freud. David knows, though, that Danny will seek him out to discuss what he's read, and he says that he'll recommend other psychology books so that he doesn't think that Freud is the end-all, be-all of the field.

On the next Shabbat, Reuven agrees to meet Danny and Reb to study Talmud. He makes his way into Danny's neighborhood, but being only three o'clock, no one but playing children are out in the street, and the synagogue is empty. He calls up the stairs to Danny, who introduces Reuven to his sister and mother. Reuven finds Danny's sister pretty—she smiles at him and tells him that Danny talks of him often—and he sees that the women are studying a Yiddish book in the living room. The fact that Danny's sister is never named is noteworthy; women are so non-existent or invisible in the novel—and by extension in the culture—that they do not even seem to merit a name. As one critic noted, "Danny's mother is almost a nonentity in the novel, and thus a reader might conclude that the author's unconscious dictated the neutralization or elimination of the mother as a means of facilitating peace between fathers and sons—and even within male society when male fraternal bonding is based on the putting down of women" (Sternlicht 46)

Reuven and Danny head to the third floor, where Danny's room, a conference room, and his father's study are. Reuven notices that the walls throughout the home are white and bare, with no photographs or paintings of any kind. Potok emphasizes yet again, through this detail, how stripped down and bare the life of a Hasid is; although the judgment, or at the very least pity, appears in Reuven's narration, Potok's own struggle regarding the lack of place for art in Jewish history and culture seems to gain voice in such moments.

The boys knock on the study door and enter a room packed with books. They sit on each side of Reb, who asks about Reuven's eye. Reuven tells him it doesn't hurt, but he still can't read. Reb tells Reuven he can simply listen, then, and says that although he knows Reuven's a good mathematician, he wants to see what Reuven knows more important things. Reb smiles, and Reuven wonders how he will fare. He knows that in breadth, he cannot match Danny and Reb, but his depth of knowledge concerning certain passages is his strength. David, Reuven explains, prefers to study this way—wherein one exhaustively studies one part before moving on to another—and has trained his son to do so also. The ideal, Reuven admits, is to study both ways—to study as much as one can in as much depth as one can—but because of the yeshiva's emphasis on English studies, Reuven explains, it seemed an impossible ideal.

The study begins, and Reuven and Danny take turns explaining passages after Reb reads them aloud, but Danny and his father soon venture into a pitched battle that has none of the quietness or restraint of the previous one. He notices that there is a closeness, an ease with each other, that had not been present at the service. Danny wins only slightly more often than his father, and Reuven notices that Reb seems happier when he loses than when he wins, demonstrating a deep affection for, and pride in, his son.

Reuven also notices that as they argue, they both occasionally throw looks his way, as if wondering why he's not taking part. Finally, he joins in, and soon he's enjoying himself so much that he reads from a book before Reb stops him, reminding him that he isn't supposed to read. An argument soon ensues between Danny and Reuven over commentaries, and Reb sits and listens quietly. The argument ends in a draw, and Reb asks Danny to go get tea for them all.

After Danny leaves, Reb says that he knows Reuven has a good head, but that he wants to see if he also has a good soul. Reb tells Reuven that he knows that Danny spends his afternoons in the library, sometimes with Reuven, sometimes with his father, and he wants to know what he reads. He says he would ask Danny himself, but it's hard for him to talk to his son. Reuven, shocked into silence, thinks about how his own father gave Danny books behind Reb's back, and how Reb was now interrogating him behind Danny's back, illuminating the fractured father-son pairing that's occurring in the novel as a result of secrets. Reuven slowly recounts everything about Danny's visits to the library, choosing to omit the parts about learning German, reading Freud, and studying Jewish histories that were less than complimentary regarding the Hasidim.

When Reuven finishes, Reb covers his face with his hand and rocks back and forth, muttering about Darwin and psychology, both of which epitomize secular, modern modes of learning and belief. Reb cannot speak to his son, he says, though God gave him a brilliant child. Reb voices his hope that Reuven and David will be good influences on Danny, and that Reuven will not make a goy of him. Reuven shakes his head.

Reb looks to the ceiling, plaintively crying out that God made his son too brilliant, when he and Reuven hear a door, then the clicks of Danny's metal-capped shoes. Reb composes himself, and Danny re-enters the study, carrying a tray with tea and cookies. Reuven isn't sure what he'll tell Danny when they're alone, though he notes that Reb said nothing about keeping their exchange a secret. Wanting to talk with his father about what happened, Reuven hopes Danny will not ask him that day.

Reb finishes his tea and crosses his arms, then resumes discussion about the Talmud, as if nothing happened. They go to services, and then Danny offers to walk Reuven part of the way home. Naturally, of course, he asks about what happened. Reuven tells him everything, and Danny appears not at all surprised by his father's knowledge. Danny just wishes his father had just asked him. Reuven questions this strange silence between father and son again. In response, Danny says that when he was ten or eleven, he had gone to his father and complained about something, at which point Reb told him to shut his mouth and look into his soul. From this point on, he understood that he was supposed to look inside himself for the answers instead of running to his father.

Though Danny feels some relief, since he no longer has to feel scared in the library, he doesn't understand his father's silence toward him. The boys get frustrated with each other—Danny can't make Reuven understand his position, and Reuven doesn't understand why Danny can't thwart these constraints—and Danny turns to walk back home, muttering "good night."

Reuven's father is shocked by the nature of Danny and Reb's relationship, which Reuven describes upon coming home. David alludes to something he once heard about in Russia but hadn't believed. He won't elucidate any more, though, when Reuven asks, but rather says he's glad Reb knows about the library. Reuven asks why Reb can't talk to Danny about it, and David says that he has—through Reuven.

The next day, Reuven comes home and gets help from his father, who reads aloud from Reuven's textbooks; the next morning, he goes to Dr. Snydman, who tells Reuven and his father that the eye has healed perfectly, and that Reuven is free to do anything he wishes again (**Chapter Nine**). Both father and son cry with relief on the way to the school. Reuven remembers that he meant to ask Dr. Snydman about Billy, but he decides to call Billy later in the week and visit him.

At this point, the school has an exam week, but this doesn't bother Reuven, since the newness of holding a pen and reading energizes him. He doesn't see Danny but talks with him by phone mid-week, and the mention of this demonstrates how close the two have already become. Reuven asks about Danny's summer plans, but Danny says he'll just be studying the Talmud and Freud. Reuven makes plans to visit him that Shabbat.

Reuven's last exam happens Friday, freeing him for the summer. After lunch—during which Reuven and David discuss the war—Reuven looks up Billy's father in the phone book. Reuven calls but finds out, from Billy's dad, that Billy's surgery hadn't been successful. Mr. Merrit asks how Reuven's eye is, and after he tells Billy's father it healed, Reuven asks if he could visit Billy. Merrit says he's in Albany, with friends, and that he himself is moving to Albany today. Mr. Merrit cautions Reuven to be careful with his eyes, and they hang up. This call upsets Reuven, who sits in his room, wanders around the apartment, and sits on the porch. From the corner of his eye, Reuven spots a spider spinning a web in the corner of the porch rail. A housefly is caught in it but still alive, its legs kicking. It manages to get its wings free, but while struggling to free its body, the wings get wound in the web again. The spider works its way across the web to the fly, and Reuven approaches the web. The fly gets its wings free again, but the body is stuck. Reuven blows air against the web, but it only sways. He tries again, and the web's strands unravel, leaving the fly on the porch floor. It soon flies away, and the spider disappears.

So much attention is given this last image that Potok clearly intends for it to be a symbol. On its own, the fly becomes more trapped the more it struggles, and it takes Reuven's intervention to set it free. In this way, Danny is like the fly; he needs Reuven's help to escape his fate.

In **Chapter Ten**, Danny and Reuven see each other almost every day during the first month of the summer. Danny spends morning studying the Talmud alone or with his father, while Reuven plays ball during three mornings a week, then studies Talmud with his father for three mornings; this detail contrasts the level of expectations that lie on the two boys' shoulders. While Reuven and David Malter often only work on ten lines at a time, Danny's father increases his son's daily Talmud goal to three blatt (pages). Despite this, Danny still spends every afternoon in the library, where Reuven meets up with him. Sometimes David Malter comes, too, working on an article that requires research. Reuven invites Danny to supper once, but Mr. Malter later explains to Reuven that because of kashruth (religion-based eating restrictions), Danny can only eat at his home, or the home of one of his father's followers—a fact that highlights the closed-off nature of Danny's Hasid community.

Reuven spends Shabbat afternoons doing battle over the Talmud with Reb and Danny before services. The evenings are unscheduled, and though Danny and Reuven often spend them together, too, Danny can't go to movies because his father forbids it—another restriction to protect him from secular society. Meanwhile, the war rages on, and Reuven adds more maps from the *New York Times* onto his wall. He mentions specific military maneuvers that occur during this summer, including preparation for an invasion of occupied France. Reuven and his father listen to the radio, read newspapers, and study maps, and though the journalists seem to put a positive spin on things, the Malters are worried by the Allies' slow progress and the weather. All these details, of course, highlight Reuven's awareness and engagement with the "outside world" while holding it up against its opposite—that is, the willfully contained, insulated world of the Hasidim, who wish to pretend, as much as possible, that an outside world doesn't exist, or, at the very least, won't affect them. (The novel's readers, of course, know that the truth regarding Nazi concentration camps is soon to be revealed, and thus already have the sense that the Hasidim's defense-mechanism ideals will confront an even harder test than that which American society itself has presented.)

In late July, to research his article, Mr. Malter travels each afternoon, for a week, to Manhattan; Reuven lunches with him on these days, then leaves to meet Danny at the library, and it is during this time that Danny begins to read Freud in its original German. He struggles, though; not only with the language, but with the complicated ideas and terminology. Reuven, meanwhile, tries to read a complicated book on mathematics before giving up on it and re-reading the article on symbolic logic that he'd tried to read before, as well as a book on the same subject. By Thursday, Danny's table is covered with stacks of books, and he looks miserable, pronouncing the pursuit impossible. Even the English translations confuse him, as the basis of the translation often seems ambiguous. He leaves, disgusted and angry, and when Reuven sees him again that Shabbat, Danny's mood has not improved. The Talmudic battle resumes as it had on previous Shabbats, with Danny taking his place as an enthusiastic participant.

Danny's quiet while walking Reuven home, saying he'll see him at the library the next day just before turning to go home. The next day, Reuven finds Danny in his usual spot, smiling, and there are three books open on his table: a German-English dictionary, a volume of Freud's early papers, and a dictionary of psychological terms. Danny said that he had to approach Freud like the Talmud—that is, with commentary. Freud couldn't be read, he argued. He had to be studied, sentence by sentence. In this way, as noted by many scholars, psychology becomes Danny's religion, seemingly replacing Judaism—the precise thing Reb fears. Not only does Danny have a godhead in Freud, but he approaches his texts in the same way one does the Talmud, thus making the association between Danny's new secular religion and Judaism all the more tangible.

Later that week, Reuven tells Danny that he and his father

will be leaving for a month to stay in a cottage near the Peekskills. Reuven gives Danny two books he thinks he'd like: *The Making of the Modern Jew* and *The Nineteen Letters of Ben Uzziel*. By the time Reuven leaves, Danny is through the first of Freud's papers and working on the second. Danny and Reuven agree not to write—they feel it's too childish when they'll be separated only a month—and Reuven doesn't see Danny until Labor Day.

As soon as Reuven returns, he calls Danny, and though he's not at home—he's in Lakewood with his father, visiting a family friend—he calls Reuven back that night, telling of his miserable experience. He'd spent hours on a bus with his father, silent but for an occasional Talmud discussion. Danny tells Reuven, with some bitterness, how lucky he is to be able to talk with his father.

The next day, in the library, Danny tells Reuven he enjoyed the books on contemporary Judaism. Reb hadn't been pleased about Danny bringing such books into his house, but Reb softened when Danny told him the books came from Reuven. Danny had also read a lot more of Freud, and he wants to discuss with Reuven a shocking paper he read about sexuality, since he doesn't feel there's anyone else with whom he could talk about it. Reuven notes, though, that although they'd planned to discuss it that Shabbat, they never did, and then school began again. Reuven becomes so busy that he can't even think about, let alone discuss, Freud's writings.

The two boys' senior year is so busy that for two months, they only see each other on Shabbat afternoons (**Chapter Eleven**). Reuven's elected president of his class, and though he talks with Danny by phone often, he can't visit him during the week until November; by then, Danny looks tired and says he doesn't go to the library much anymore because of his workload. Reuven asks about his Freud research, and Danny says that what he read has upset him. He wants to have a long talk with Reuven about his findings, but they both get busier and it never happens. Potok's repeated avoidance of this sex-themed discussion between the characters isn't surprising; when the conversation finally happens, it occurs off-stage, and it's dismissed quickly. Thus, despite the fact that *The Chosen* is a bildungsroman, or coming-of-age novel, sexuality is an element that's noticeably absent. Though Reuven once mentions he's dating, and finds Danny's unnamed sister attractive, and Danny expects an arranged marriage, Potok generally steers away from the topic, presumably thinking that it would detract attention from the intellectual, religious conflict that anchors the story. Predictably, though, when Hollywood pursued a film project based on the novel, the attraction between Reuven and Danny's sister received much more attention.

In December of the boys' senior year, the Battle of the Bulge begins, and American casualties rise. In the evenings, Reuven studies in his room, hearing radio reports while following along with his maps. The battle ends in January, with huge death tolls on both sides, and during this time Danny and Reuven only speak by phone. Danny reports that his brother had gotten worse, but that he went to the hospital and seemed better, thanks to some pills. Danny urges Reuven to visit, but Reuven can't find the time.

After mid-year exams in February, Reuven visits his friend, but they only engage in a Talmudic discussion with Reb Saunders and never get the chance to talk alone. In the larger world, the Russians and Americans are advancing, and the end of the war seemed imminent. The news excites Reuven, and even Reb and Danny, both of whom seem generally disengaged from world issues. Rumors of the war's end circulate as Danny is laid up with the flu in late March and bronchitis in early April. Because of illness, Danny can neither see nor speak with Reuven.

At this time, Reuven has a student government meeting that's broken up by Davey Cantor, who tells them all that F.D.R. has died. The meeting adjourns, and Reuven, in shock, steps outside. He catches a trolley, wherein a woman weeps and no one speaks. Reuven finds himself crying, feeling as though his own father has died. (Thus, once again, father-son relationships of various kinds resonate and echo, while world events' direct affect on characters' lives foreshadows the consequences of future Holocaust revelations.)

When Reuven reaches home, he finds Manya crying, making dinner, and David listening to the radio in the kitchen. Harry Truman is now president, and Reuven wonders at how Roosevelt's death came when America was about to win the war. The family eats dinner with the radio on that night and leaves it on throughout the weekend, excepting Shabbat. Because Danny is still too sick to even come to the phone, Reuven spends Shabbat with David, with whom he goes to services and, later, discusses Roosevelt. David sobs with grief and leaves Reuven's room to be alone. Reuven thinks about the unfairness of Roosevelt's death, comparing it with Billy's misfortune, and he cries until he falls asleep.

Roosevelt's funeral occurs the following day, so schools close, and Reuven and his father listen to the radio all day. Following the funeral, Danny calls. Though still sick, he no longer has a fever, though his brother is now sick. Danny wants Reuven to visit, but Reuven contracts a high fever of his own, thus requiring him to stay in bed for ten days. This overwhelming presence of illness among the main characters throughout the novel indicates how the body can respond to external stresses. In this case, both Danny and Reuven's defenses seem weakened by bad news and/or anxiety about their lives.

When Reuven returns to school, he's so overwhelmed by catching up that he temporarily drops his student government commitments. By May, Reuven finally catches up, though both his father and Reb Saunders fall ill at this time, and the war in Europe finally ends. Though this is, at first, a time of great joy for Reuven and David, only a few days pass before they learn the truth about the concentration camps. David breaks down, weeping, and asks Reuven to leave him alone; he does, going to his room to ponder the senselessness of millions of Jews' murder.

Reuven goes to Danny's on the Shabbat, but instead of battling over the Talmud, Reb talks about his childhood in Russia, the Cossacks, and the people he had known that were probably dead. While Danny and Reuven sit quietly, both nervous, Reb says, again and again, that their suffering must be God's will, though he asks God, in one momentary crisis of faith, how He could allow such a thing to happen. In this moment, readers witness Reb's crisis of faith, even though he ultimately comes round to his original pessimistic, but understandable, belief: Jews are meant to suffer on earth.

Danny has too much work to walk Reuven home, so he goes alone, finds his father listening to the radio in his bedroom, and joins him. David asks about Reb; when Reuven mentions how Reb asked God how He could let something like this happen, David grows agitated, asking if God answered him. Reuven explains Reb's belief in God's will, and David asks Reuven if that answer satisfies him. He says no, and David agrees, saying that they cannot wait for God but must instead act for themselves, in order to give meaning to the death of so many Jews. He says that because of Hitler, only American Jewry remains, and this thrusts a terrible responsibility on them all. In David's view, if Jewry in America is not re-built and made to flourish, then they, as a people, will die out.

David doesn't return to teaching until the end of May, and two days after Reuven's exams, David has a heart attack. (Regarding the symbolic role of illness in the novel, David's heart, in this chapter, appears to literally break upon hearing the news of the Holocaust.) At first, while he stays in the hospital, Reuven stays at home with Manya, but soon, Reb calls and suggests that Reuven stay with the Saunders, sharing Danny's room, until David is released. David tells Reuven to accept the offer—an offer through which Potok shows readers that Reb is not simply a stubborn, monolithic, mean-spirited tyrant, but rather a man just as capable of compassion as he is of cruelty.

The Saunders accept Reuven as part of their family in **Chapter Twelve**. Danny's mother, weakened by an unnamed heart condition—yet another illness in the novel—adds food to Reuven's plate; Danny's pretty sister teases the boys; Danny's brother, Levi, picks at his food and wanders around the house like a ghost; and Reb occasionally suffers spontaneous bouts of weeping, which lead him to leave the room. No one speaks of these outbursts, which frightens and bewilders Reuven.

For that month, though, he and Danny are constantly

together. They would visit David in the hospital each day at four, join the Saunders for dinner, and then either hang out with Danny's mother and sister, read, or participate in Talmudic battles with Reb. The latter happened seldom, though, since Reb's time was so occupied. People constantly came to speak with him, and by dinner, he always looks fatigued. Reuven notices that throughout the month, Reb and Danny do not, indeed, speak to each other at all outside of Talmudic study, and their incapacity to talk to each other troubles him.

At the library each afternoon, Reuven and Danny talk of Freud. The readings disturb and upset Danny, but he can't stop consuming them because he feels that Freud possesses an uncanny insight regarding man's nature. Though Freud's vision of man is not complimentary, and not at all religious—indeed, it tears "man from God, as Danny put it, and marrie[s] him off to Satan"—Danny is exhilarated by the ideas. He's become comfortable with the field's technical jargon, and he spends a good deal of time explaining Freud's main ideas to Reuven. Naturally, he becomes upset, too, and wonders how two such contradictory philosophies—that of Freud and that of the Talmud—could simultaneously be absorbed and co-exist in Danny's mind: a reduction of the novel's central question. Reuven voices this concern, but Danny merely shrugs and returns to his reading.

If David was well, Reuven would speak to him about this, but he's recuperating slowly and is already upset regularly by reading Holocaust articles voraciously. He speaks constantly about the American Jew's responsibility, as well as about the role of Palestine as a Jewish nation. Once, he asks the boys what they're reading, and Danny answers truthfully: Freud. Reuven's afraid that his father is going to argue with Danny, but David just shakes his head, says he's tired, and tells Danny that he'll speak to him of Freud another time. David tells Danny that Freud is fallible, and that many others disagree with his ideas—clearly trying to discourage Danny's "worship" of Freud—but then David raises the topic of European Jewry again. He tells Reuven and Danny that the English knew the

Nazis' plan but failed to act, and that they, along with Americans and others, had not cared enough. For this reason, David argues, Jews can wait no longer for God to act, and they must make Palestine a Jewish homeland. Such discussions upset David, but he can speak of nothing else.

At breakfast one morning, Reb tells Reuven a story of a Hasid who journeyed to Palestine, planning to spend his last years in the Holy Land. The man reached the Wailing Wall in Jerusalem, and three days later, while praying at the Wall for the Messiah to come, he died. Without mentioning his father, Reuven mentions that many people think Palestine should become a Jewish homeland now, rather than simply being a place to which Jews journeyed to die. Everyone at the Saunders' table freezes, and Reb angrily, he asks who these people are, insisting that Palestine won't truly be a homeland for Jews until God makes it so. Reb's rage surprises Reuven into silence.

Reb asks Reuven whether Jews should just forget about the Messiah, and whether this abomination was what six million Jews died for. Reb says he brought his people from Russia to America because he thought it better to live in a land of true goyim than in a land of Jewish goyim. True Jews would never suggest making Palestine a homeland now, according to Reb. This exchange emphasizes that although there were clear distinctions and hostilities between sects of Jews before, the Holocaust, ironically, caused more and greater fissures to grow between them.

Danny's sister tries to calm Reb, and Reuven apologizes. Danny's sister says that Reuven didn't speak for himself when Reb stops her with a gesture, performs the Grace, and leaves the kitchen. Reuven's assessment of Reb as a tyrant seems apropos in this scene.

Later, when the boys are in Danny's room, Danny warns Reuven that his father loses his temper whenever he's confronted with an idea that he thinks comes from "the contaminated world." Reuven says he didn't know that Zionism fell into this category, and Danny tells Reuven not to talk of it any longer, explaining that in his father's estimation, a secular

Jewish state is a sacrilege and a violation of the Torah. Reuven says he's glad he hadn't mentioned that the view was his father's, and Danny says that Reb would have thrown him out of the house if Reuven had. Thus, in this passage, the seeds for deep conflict between the two families are planted; world events have trickled down to affect the lives of two adolescent friends.

Reuven asks about Reb's crying fits, and Danny explains that Reb's thinking of, and suffering for, the six million Jews who died—an important idea that will re-appear later in the novel. Reuven says he doesn't feel like studying the Talmud that morning and wants to take a walk. Later, at lunch, Reb is back to normal, but Reuven will be extra-careful with his words from that point forward.

One afternoon late in July, at the library, Danny talks of his little brother. Though half Danny's age, Levi gets glasses, for reasons that have nothing to do with reading too much. Danny says Levi's a good kid, despite the handicap his illness imposes. He's bright, and he studies, but Reb cannot pressure Levi because of his weakness. Danny surprises Reuven by saying that Levi would make a good tzaddik. As hints have previously indicated, Danny desperately wants Levi to inherit the family position, thus freeing Danny to pursue his secular interests and studies.

Reuven confirms that Danny hasn't suggested this to Reb (and jokes that he wants to be out of town when Danny does). Danny says that he'll need Reuven that day, confessing that his concern for Levi is rooted in self-interest, not a strong relationship. Reuven tries to change the subject to Danny's sister, but Danny stays focused on Reb. Danny admires him—though he still doesn't understand his choice regarding their silence—and trusts him, and pities him. He understands that his father was born trapped into his fate, and Danny is becoming more aggressive about planning his own escape.

Danny says that his sister was promised to the son of one of Reb's followers when she was two years old. She'll marry him when she turns eighteen. Scholars who criticize Potok's bleak portrayal of this suffocating Hasidic community point to this as an error that flirts with propaganda; according to them, a girl who reached that age would ultimately have the power to veto the marriage if she found her fiancee to be unsatisfactory.

Danny suggests that he and Reuven go visit David at the hospital; this is the only time they ever discuss Danny's sister.

The next week, David and Reuven head to their cottage near the Peekskill. During their stay, America drops atomic bombs on Hiroshima and Nagasaki, ending the war with Japan. Reuven doesn't tell his father about his conversation with Danny, but he has nightmares all month about Reb Saunders blaming him for his son's defection, indicating Reuven's guilty conscience. In September, the boys start classes at Hirsch College, raising the stakes once again; for Danny cannot help but be more tempted by, and more exposed to, the studies and ideas that lead him further away from his Hasidic rootings.

At the beginning of **Book Three, Chapter Thirteen,** Danny is miserable. After only a week of college, he discovers that the psychology department chair, Professor Appleman, favors experimental psychology and has "an intense distaste for psychoanalysis in general and for Freud in particular." The two young men meet in front of Reuven's synagogue each morning to take the trolley to school, during which time Danny complains about Appleman, his textbook, and rats in mazes. Frustrated, Danny doesn't understand what such experiments tell him about the mind.

The school is concentrated in one large building and stands near a Catholic church, adorned by a large crucifix; Hirsch students are confronted with this Christian symbol daily, indicating how much closer they all are to the day when they must confront the mainstream, largely Christian, American culture. A "rigidly Orthodox school," Hirsch has services three times a day, and from nine to three o'clock, students study the Talmud. After that, for three or four hours, they study other subjects. The days are long and demanding, and Reuven admits that although he enjoys his classes, he often must stay up until 1:00 a.m. in order to finish his homework. Danny, meanwhile, grows more and more distempered, despite the fact that his peers in Rav Gershenson's class—the most prestigious in the school (Reuven's in the next-highest)—look at him in wonder. Soon, Danny becomes the unofficial arbiter of student disputes, as well as the leader of the Hasidic students. This fails to make him happy, however, as he still broods over Professor Appleman and his psychology program. Thus discouraged, Danny considers pursuing a different course of study, and earns a "B" in his psychology class due to some botched math equations on his final exam.

Reuven suggests that Danny talk to Appleman, but Danny says that the one time he mentioned Freud in class, Appleman made a speech about how psychoanalysis was related to psychology in the same way that magic was related to science. The professor criticized Freud's followers for being too interested in dubious theoreticals that can't be tangibly tested or refuted.

Reuven quietly remarks that he thinks Appleman's right; if Freudians aren't willing to put their theories to the test, they're being dogmatic. Danny grows angry, arguing that Freud was a scientist. Reuven reiterates that Danny should talk to Appleman, and Danny finally agrees, saying he can't be made more miserable than he is now. Significantly, Danny's resistance to speak with Appleman can be connected to the silence he lives in at home. He's become accustomed to fuming alone, and swallowing his frustrations, to such an extent that rather than face rejection or denial of his new "religion," he prefers to wallow in anger. Ironically, of course, this makes Danny a tyrannical zealot not unlike his father, though the religions to which the two stubbornly adhere are now utterly different.

Reuven asks Danny about his eyes; the doctor said that the glasses Danny got when he began college should solve his problems. Danny adds that he'll talk to Appleman the following week, and the worst that will happen is he'll drop his course. He asks Reuven if he plans to come over for Shabbat this week, and Reuven declines, explaining that he will be studying Talmud with his father. Danny says that his father asked the previous week whether or not the two boys were still friends, since he hadn't seen Reuven in two months. But

Reuven explains that he's learning scientific method from David. Danny grins and asks if Reuven plans to unleash scientific method on Rav Schwartz, his Talmud teacher.

Reuven doesn't think Schwartz would welcome scientific method in class, since Reuven's previous class contribution of a textual emandation led to a "queer look" from the old teacher. Danny gets up to leave and warns Reuven not to try scientific method on Gershenson, who "knows all about it and hates it." He asks when Reb will get to see Reuven, and Reuven responds that he doesn't know. He asks whether Danny and his father are talking now, and Danny says, "Only now and then. It's not really talking." With that, Danny heads down the street toward home.

David stands in the doorway of his study. He has had three colds in five months, and this is the first time in weeks that he's been home in the evening as a result of his new, all-consuming passion regarding Zionism. He raises money, teaches adult education courses, attends meetings, and makes speeches each night, then comes home exhausted. He has tea, talks to Reuven for a few minutes in his room, and leaves to prepare for the next day's classes. But this night, he asks Reuven what Danny had been so excited about, having heard the young man's voice through the door. Reuven tells him about Danny's difficulties with Professor Appleman, as well as Reuven's advice about meeting with Appleman to discuss the problem. Reuven says that Appleman sounds like his empiricist logic teacher, Professor Flesser, and his father asks why. Reuven explains that each believes that in order for a science to be valid, its theories must be provable by experimentation and mathematics.

David urges his son to sleep, and Reuven inquires about his father's health, asking whether or not Dr. Grossman knows he's working so hard, and if his father has a check-up scheduled in the near future. Mr. Malter reassures Reuven that he's fine, but that it's not the time to take it easy, making reference to two Jewish groups in Palestine: the Irgun and the Haganah. The Irgun was a Jewish terrorist group who kidnapped British officials in order to gain leverage when bargaining with the British army and government; the Haganah, though, concentrated on smuggling more Jews into Palestine, despite the fact that Britain had officially sealed its borders. Though David hates the violence of the Irgun, he hates the British non-immigration policy more, and his dismay and sadness fuels his exhaustive efforts.

Reuven, seeing that his father's getting worked up, changes the subject to Reb, saying that he's wondering why he no longer sees Reuven. After a long silence, David asks his son if he knows what the rabbis say God said to Moses when he died: "He said to Moses, 'You have toiled and labored, now you are worthy of rest.'" A human life is finite and quick, David says, and one wonders why a person must suffer so much when an individual's life is irrelevant in the face of eternity. But, David argues, although a life span, in and of itself, comes to nothing, the man who lives that life *is* something. A man must fill his life with meaning—meaning does not automatically come with life—but such infusion takes much work. David wants to be worthy of rest when he dies, and giving his life meaning will insure that.

Reuven's shaken by this discussion of his death. David apologizes for his bluntness, assuring Reuven that he will live many more years to come. But he wants to convey why he's doing what he is doing. Reuven has a hard time shaking his dread and discomfort, making David promise to visit his doctor the following week. David agrees, then changes the subject to divert Reuven: he tells him that Jack Rose—a successful, wealthy furrier who grew up with David in Russia, though the man had since become an unobservant Jew—contributed one thousand dollars to the Jewish National Fund, even though he had contributed the same amount to David's synagogue six months before. David says strange things are happening, a kind of religious renaissance, wherein even Jack Rose has joined a temple to provide his grandchildren with a Jewish education. Reuven's surprised, as he had regarded Jack's utter abandonment of Judaism distasteful—so much so that he had asked his father why they remained friends. The question upsets David, who says that "honest differences of opinion should never be permitted to destroy a friendship," thus forecasting the test that lies ahead for Reuven and Danny. But Reuven merely thinks about how Jack Rose is assuaging his feelings of guilt by giving money, and he voices the idea that he doesn't envy Jack Rose's rabbi. David asks why not, telling Reuven that more people are returning to their faith, and that the rabbis must educate them, just as Reuven must when he becomes a rabbi.

Smiling, David remarks that he would have liked to see Reuven pursue a career as a college professor, but Reuven has decided to be a rabbi, even if his synagogue is full of Jack Roses. The two men have tea and discuss David's Zionist activity, as well as the media coverage of Palestine. David insists that events will come to a bloody, violent head in one or two years, if Britain does not hand the reins over to the United Nations. Only the Jews who read the Yiddish press know the full story, David claims, and he tells Reuven of a large rally, scheduled for February in Madison Square Garden, that his group has planned and will advertise in the *New York Times*. Reuven wonders aloud what Reb will think of Danny being friends with the son of a prominent Zionist (Reuven had told David about Reb's fury regarding the topic). David says Reb wants to wait for the Messiah, but David is tired of waiting and wants to bring the Messiah.

It's Friday now, and Reuven has no plans. Danny is studying with his father, so Reuven wakes up late and heads to the college library by trolley. He looks at books about experimental psychology, and he soon understands Danny's misery. The books are full of charts, graphs, tables, lab findings, and mathematical results of experiments. Freud is nowhere to be found, even in bibliographies. Reuven looks up "unconscious" in the indices, but only finds disparaging remarks about its unscientific foundation and its comparisons to magic, reminding Reuven of Appleman. It makes sense to Reuven that in order for something to have scientific validity, it must be able to be tested and proven. Despite his own bias, however, he pities how Danny's mind is being tortured by Appleman at school while Danny's soul is being tortured by Reb's silence at home.

The following Monday, the college semester begins, and Danny tells Reuven at lunch that he plans on speaking with Appleman that afternoon. Reuven encourages him, but also tells him that he believes, after looking at the library books, that experimental psychology has a lot to offer. This angers Danny, who sarcastically thanks Reuven and leaves. Though the two usually go home together, Danny doesn't show, though he waits by Reuven's synagogue the next morning. Danny explains that he and Appleman had a long talk, and—after apologizing to Reuven—he declares Appleman a fine man; the professor had been waiting all year for Danny to come in and speak with him. Appleman knows a lot about Freud, Danny explains, and it's not the man's conclusions Appleman objects to, but rather his methodology—basing generalized theories only on the basis of his own personal experiences and those of a few patients. Reuven offers that that's the problem of induction in a nutshell: how many confirmations are necessary before one can make a generalization?

Danny says that Appleman also made the point that while Freud concentrated solely on abnormal cases, experimental psychology tries to discover how all humans behave. Appleman has a problem with Freudians more than Freud, Danny tells Reuven, as they are paid huge fees and refuse to test their ideas and methods. Danny and Reuven board the trolley for school, and everyone stares at Danny's earlocks, fringes, and beard. (Danny has become more self-conscious about his appearance since reading Graetz's work on the Hasidim, Reuven notes.) Once they're settled, Danny says that he and Appleman discussed experimental psychology, and why animals are easier to experiment with than humans. Echoing David, Appleman told Danny that Freud wasn't God, and argued that since religious people argue about the nature of God, it just made sense that scientists took issue with each other, too. Appleman tells Danny that learning about experimental psychology will be good for him, though Danny's skeptical, and will provide a balance for his knowledge of Freud. This idea is an important one; Potok champions balance, most significantly in terms of tradition and assimilation—the Malters are the ideal—but even

Appleman's plea to Danny for balance in his studies demonstrates a need for more open-mindedness. Near the end of their conversation, the professor offers to help Danny with the math, but because the teacher's time is limited, he suggests that Danny find a peer to help him also.

Reuven starts coaching Danny regularly in math, and not surprisingly, Reuven learns about experimental psychology along the way, finding it fascinating and more substantial than Freud. Danny is an able student, though he primarily memorizes and concentrates on the "how" rather than wondering about the "why." The two sit in the lunchroom, at their own table, and work, and Reuven occasionally argues the value of experimentation. Though still skeptical, Danny comes to acknowledge its worth in certain contexts.

David Malter, meanwhile, is never home except for breakfast, supper, and Shabbat. As before, he comes into Reuven's room late at night to talk, but he gets little sleep. Though his doctor had given him a clean bill of health, he urged David to get more rest. He doesn't, though, of course, and when Reuven brings up the subject, David talks about the violence in Palestine and, thus, the urgency of his quest. Only two things now matter to him: the education of American Jews and the establishment of a Jewish state. In this way, David's absorption into the Zionist cause mirrors the fanaticism of Reb Saunders.

Thoughts about Zionism vary widely on the Hirsch College campus. The Revisionists supported the Irgun, while the Neturai Karta, or Guardians of the City (Jerusalem), despise all efforts to establish a Jewish state before the arrival of the Messiah. Most in this latter group, like Reb Saunders, are "severely Orthodox Jews," and on campus, they became a "small but highly vocal element of the school's student population." The rabbis are split, and the college faculty are all in favor of a Jewish state. Discussions about the problem of dual allegiances, to America and Israel, arise, with the end question being: "On what side would an American Jew fight should America ever declare war against a Jewish state?" Reuven dismisses this question, saying that America would never ask Jews to fight Jews, citing a World War II example: Japanese American soliders had been sent to fight Germans, not the Japanese. Reuven's answer never satisfies them, however, and he explains to readers that most of the heated debates occur among those who believed in pursuing a Jewish state; those who didn't, like the Hasidim, didn't even bother with questions and hypotheticals. To them, such discussions were "bitul Torah," or wasted time that should have been spent studying the Torah.

In February, the ranks of the different factions grow and become more defined, as each group recruits students. Reuven joins a religious Zionist group. One day at lunch, a Hasid accuses a Revisionist of being worse than Hitler, who had only destroyed the Jewish body, whereas the Revisionists were destroying the Jewish soul. A fistfight almost resulted, and the incident polarized the groups even more profoundly. Not surprisingly, Danny doesn't join any group, though he secretly confesses to Reuven that he would like to join his. Danny's position is tricky: the anti-Zionists see him as their leader, so he again feels trapped by Hasidic culture. He says nothing during debates, Reuven notes, and when the incident in the lunchroom occurs, he only scowls darkly at the Hasid who started the conflict.

In the third week of February, news breaks about the British Foreign Minister's plans to bring up the Palestine issue at the United Nations, and David Malter is thrilled, though this forces him to change his rally speech. He practices it in front of Reuven one Shabbat, and Reuven feels proud of his father, moved by the speech. The day before the rally, though, it snows all day, and the streets are still covered in snow when David leaves for the rally. Reuven must stay home to study for a logic exam, but he has trouble concentrating, imagining his father standing in front of empty seats. He studies the best he can and wanders around the apartment. Just before one o'clock, he hears the door and rushes to the hall. Excited, David tells him that Madison Square Garden had been filled, with two thousand people standing outside, listening to the speeches through loudspeakers. The two stay up until three talking about the rally's success.

The next day, all the New York newspapers feature articles on the rally, and the Yiddish papers quote David's speech extensively, thus making Reuven the target of Hirsch's anti-Zionists and the hero of the movement's supporters. He barely notices Danny's absence that day at lunch, and because of his distractedness and fatigue, his exam doesn't go well, but he's not troubled by this. At the day's end, he waits more than a half hour for Danny, but he never comes, and Reuven heads home alone. The next morning, Danny fails to arrive again, and at school, while Reuven prepares for his Talmud session, Danny walks past and motions, with his head, for Reuven to follow. He does, and Danny leads him to the bathroom, which is empty. Reb read about David's role in the rally, Danny explains, and as a result, he forbade Danny from seeing, speaking to, listening to, or being within four feet of, Reuven. Furthermore, if Reb ever learned of Danny associating with Reuven again, he would pull him from college and send him to an out-of-town yeshiva for rabbinic ordination. Even this private moment in the bathroom is risky, but Danny says that he had to tell Reuven. Just then, a Hasid comes in and chooses the urinal furthest away from Reuven. Danny leaves, and when Reuven goes back out into the hall, his friend is gone.

Reuven is baffled at his excommunication not only from the Saunders' family, but also from the Hasidic students who step out of his way to avoid contact. The groups form isolated sects in the lunchroom, and Reuven once locks eyes with Danny, who looks away. Reuven is frustrated and angry about the situation, and he tells his father about it that night. David says he knew it would happen, and when Reuven says he doesn't understand why this particular offense drives the friends apart, David says that Reb likely had no choice. He could explain his son's friendship with Reuven when David was just another follower of the commandments, but as a highly visible figure in the Zionist movement, David—and by extension, his son—could no longer be viewed as harmless. David apologizes, sorry that his son's friendship with Danny has been a casualty of the cause. Reuven calls Reb a fanatic, but David counters by saying that fanatics like Reb Saunders kept Jews alive during two thousand years of exile. According to David, if the Jews in Palestine have even some of that fanaticism, they will succeed in establishing a Jewish state. Potok appears to wrestle with the idea of singleminded obsession: clearly, good can come from it—Reb's community survived, and David's call for a Jewish state is gaining recognition—but the price paid by those people's families can be enormously high.

For the rest of the semester, Danny and Reuven don't speak to each other, though they frequently make eye contact and see each other at every turn (**Chapter Fourteen**). Reuven focuses his frustration on Reb Saunders, and his schoolwork becomes a casualty of his unhappiness. Reuven tells his teachers that he's having personal problems, and he talks with his father David often, but there's nothing really to be done.

Reuven hates the silence, which makes him understand Danny's lifelong frustration on a more personal level (though Reuven also, naturally, resents how Reb has forced the exact same sort of silence upon him). Reuven hates Reb, and his feelings grow stronger when David defends the man. Though David disagrees with Reb, David nonetheless believes that ideas must be fought with ideas, not unthinking passion. Reuven maintains, however, that Reb is fighting with passion, having formed an organization that consists of Hasidic rebbes. At first, they simply hand out anti-Zionist leaflets, but the rhetoric quickly grows inflammatory, threatening local business boycotts and excommunication to those who sympathize with Zionists. They plan an anti-Zionist rally, scheduled a few days before Passover. Not many people attend, though, and scant reports on the rally detail its ugly messages.

To Reuven, the campus feels like a powder keg. A fistfight breaks out in class one day, and others are suppressed only because a new policy called for the immediate expulsion of students involved in such altercations. The conflict spills over into the students' studies, however, and Reuven notes that class arguments about unrelated topics were thinly veiled substitutes for the outlawed fistfights.

Reuven comes home after his final exams feeling deflated, having fared poorly on them, as he had his mid-terms. But his father says nothing when he sees the report card, and Reuven notes that they are both simply looking forward to spending August in the Peekskills again. There's no escape, though; before they leave, the Irgun, or Jewish terrorists, hang two innocent British officials to avenge the hanging of two of their own, and this event haunts Reuven and David to such an extent that they cut their visit short by two weeks. They head back to the city to help prepare Zionist organizations for the upcoming United Nations meeting regarding Palestine. During this time, Reuven only sees his father on Shabbat, and even then, they can no longer study Talmud together; David must rest to fortify himself, once again, for the long hours of the week ahead. Reuven worries about his father's health, but David won't listen, and Reuven's intense, prolonged isolation just makes him miss Danny—and thus, hate Reb Saunders— all the more.

In the second week of September, Reuven returns to school for registration. There, he finds himself seated a few feet from Danny, who looks at him, without a nod or an expression, and looks away. This angers Reuven, and when the semester begins two days later, he promises himself that he will forget Danny completely and not allow him to ruin another semester's grades. But this proves difficult, since Reuven is now in Rav Gershenson's Talmud class, where Danny's the star.

Gershenson teaches the Talmud like David, covering each section in great depth before moving forward. The rabbi calls on students and fires question after question at them until they fall silent, having reached the end of their memory and knowledge. At these times, Danny would usually step in and supply the answer, which Gershenson would either accept or debate, leaving the rest of the class to witness the showdown. Often, these exchanges only last a few minutes, but Reuven notes that twice, in the span of a few weeks, the Talmudic duels had gone on for more than forty-five minutes. Wryly, Reuven notes that now he, in addition to Reb Saunders, only hears Danny's voice within the context of Talmudic study.

The daily schedule allows students to review the Talmud passage between nine and twelve, eat lunch, and have class with

Gershenson from one until three. No one knows who the Rabbi will call on each day, so everyone has to prepare; but no matter what, they eventually find themselves at a loss, sitting in silence before Danny answers. All fourteen students in the class have experienced that silence, and Reuven gets a small taste of it at the beginning of October. He is stopped a moment, but as Danny raises his hand, Reuven sputters an answer to an "impossible question," and Gershenson responds, stalling Danny's intervention. In this moment, Reuven sees Danny smile slightly, and this melts Reuven's anger.

By mid-October, all the other students in the class have been called on twice, so Reuven prepares, expecting his name to be called. But weeks pass by, far into November, and although Reuven participates in class—asks questions, argues, and raises his hand as often as Danny—he begins to suspect that Gershenson, in some small way, is blacklisting Reuven to demonstrate allegiance to Reb Saunders' cause. Not only that, but Reuven's father's activities are taking a physical toll. When David comes into Reuven's room at night, the son suspects that the father isn't really listening to him, and David looks skeletal. The United Nations debate regarding the Palestine situation is underway, and daily, there's news of more bloodshed overseas, and more big rallies happen in Madison Square Garden. Reuven attends two of them, feeling great pride in his father's speeches and contributions. Reb Saunders' organization, meanwhile, distributes more leaflets, leaving them all over Reuven's school and on trolley cars.

The vote on the United Nations Partition Plan is held at the end of November, and while David's at a meeting, the vote occurs, and the Plan's passage is announced on the radio. Reuven cries at the news, and when his father returns, they hug and cry together. David feels that the Holocaust finally has meaning, and that his generation is blessed, seeing the formation of a Jewish state after two thousand years. He and Reuven talk and celebrate until three in the morning. The next day, groggy but anxious to celebrate with friends, Reuven hears on the radio, during breakfast, that a bus traveling from Tel Aviv to Jerusalem was attacked by Arabs after the vote, and that seven Jews died. This saps Reuven's joy, but upon arriving at his school, his sadness turns into fury. Reb Saunders' organizations had strewn the school with new leaflets that denounce the UN's plan, order Jews to ignore it, argue that the so-called Jewish state was a desecration of God's name, and that their organization plans to fight the new nation's recognition by the United States government.

Reuven struggles to control himself, wanting to seek out a fight and accuse the anti-Zionists, who cluster together in the halls, that they might as well consider themselves in alliance with the Arabs and the British, so opposed were they to the Jewish state. He keeps his silence, though, for which he's later grateful. For as the Arab attacks on Jews in Palestine grow in number, day by day, the anti-Zionists grow quiet and troubled, lamenting how yet more Jewish blood is being spilled. Their pain regarding these events outweighs their feelings about a Jewish state, and so a strained accord develops among the students.

Reuven receives all A's this semester, including Gershenson's class, though he's only called on once. The day after classes end, David has a second heart attack at a Jewish National Fund meeting. Rushed to the hospital, David straddles life and death for three days while Reuven worries. At the start of the next semester, though, David begins to recover. He must stay in the hospital for six weeks, and then rest for six more months before returning to work, however. When Reuven's classes resume, the students know about his father and offer condolences, and later, he sees Danny and detects masked concern on his friend's face; Reuven even thinks Danny may speak to him, but he does not. When the two pass by each other, Danny lightly touches Reuven's hand, and Reuven is comforted by this, thinking that communication between them is on its way to being restored.

At home, meanwhile, Reuven is truly alone. Though he didn't see his father much before, he saw him each night for a few minutes in his room, and without even that small bit of contact to look forward to, Reuven grows restless. He wanders the cold streets at night, and his grades begin to suffer as a result, so he pulls himself together. He sees David each day, in the early evening, and though David can barely speak, he asks if Reuven is taking care of himself. Reuven no longer fears his father's death, but rather learns to tolerate the depressing silences, trying to fill the void with Talmud study. Though he previously only studied Talmud on Shabbat and while preparing for Gershenson's class, he begins to study it each evening as well. He looks up commentaries in his father's books, and he memorizes them while also trying to anticipate Gershenson's questions. He also begins to do something he's never done: checks the cross-references of another version of the Talmud and notes the differences. (In addition to the Babylonian Talmud, the most widely used and accepted, there's also a Palestinian, or Jerusalem, Talmud; Reuven is studying the discrepancies between these two texts.)

It's now mid-February, and Gershenson still has not called on Reuven since October (yet another silence over which Reuven has no control). Because of his in-depth evening Talmud study, Reuven is days ahead of his class, and he's come upon an exceedingly difficult passage. Its gaps and holes are matched only by those found in its various commentaries, making the whole enterprise dubious, but as the class approaches this part of the text, Reuven becomes more and more certain that Gershenson will call upon him to explain this unwieldy passage. To prepare, he painstakingly re-creates the passage in its original form—the form that the authors of the commentary saw—and tries to work his way through it with the parallel text. Finally, Reuven finds a satisfying answer, and his intention is to show only his father the work with parallel texts; he plans to provide Gershenson only with the more standard, memorized response.

Of course, when the class comes to this passage, Gershenson does call on Reuven, much to the relief of his classmates (none of whom could make head nor tail of it). The Talmud is broken up into thought units, but because there's no punctuation in the Talmud, the beginnings and ends of these units are often difficult to decipher. Thanks to his study, however, Reuven knows exactly where he wishes to turn to the commentary, and he launches into his discussion as if he is a teacher himself. In detail, he lays out each part, discussing the commentary and pointing out contradictions. As he progresses, he comes to realize that he's been speaking non-stop, without any intervention from Gershenson, for an hour and a half, and the rabbi is seated at his desk, his head on his palms, listening. Soon, the bell rings, and Gershenson says nothing, dismissing the students with a wave of his hand. The next day, Reuven once again lectures on the passage without interruption for two hours, concentrating on seven words, and the third and fourth days proceed in the same manner. Reuven knows he's doing well, or else Gershenson would interrupt, but he also wishes that his teacher would say something. Reuven notices that the Hasidic students in the class stare at him now with jealousy and awe, struggling to believe that the son of a apikorsische Zionist could know the Talmud so thoroughly. Danny, though, seems happy about this turn of events; though he never looks at Reuven, Reuven sees Danny nodding and sometimes smiling as he speaks in class. Gershenson remains still, intent, and silent, and only responds with a small smile when Reuven untangles a particularly challenging point. His silence frustrates Reuven terribly, as does much of the other silences in the book.

On the fourth day, only one thought unit remains, and Reuven plans to conclude with a summary of the problems and contradictions. After he finishes, the room is silent. Gershenson, smiling slightly, stands and begins to ask Reuven some questions; after answering several, Reuven notices that it's two-thirty. But Gershenson continues, asking Reuven if one of the medieval commentaries he cited satisfies him as an answer. Not expecting this, Reuven remains silent, and even Danny, whose hand would normally shoot up at such an opportunity, sits with his mouth hanging open, obviously surprised by this question, too. Gershenson poses the question to Reuven again, and finally, the student says that it's not satisfying because it's pilpul. This stirs many in the class, and Danny shoots Reuven a quick, fearful glance. Reuven realizes that the disdain in his voice when speaking of pilpul was perhaps too obvious, and he feels suddenly self-conscious.

Gershenson remarks that Reuven obviously disapproves of

pilpul, as had a famous rabbi who opposed Hasidism in the eighteenth century. Gershenson asks why Reuven thinks its pilpul, and then asks how he, himself, explains the passage. Flustered, Reuven wonders how he should come up with an answer when none of the scholars and rabbis who came before him could not, and he tells his teacher that he can't. Gershenson prods him once more, and Reuven considers explaining how he re-constructed the original text, but then he remembers Danny telling him that Gershenson hates the critical method of studying Talmud, so he remains silent.

Gershenson sighs, admits that he cannot explain the passage himself, and that it's difficult. He closes his Talmud and dismisses the class, but asks Reuven to speak with him afterward. When all the students have gone, Gershenson asks Reuven if he studied the passage by himself, without the help of his father, and Reuven explains that his father's in the hospital recovering from a heart attack. Gershenson, surprised by this news, expresses sympathy, then asks Reuven how his father would have answered the question. Slowly, with trepidation, Reuven confesses that his father would have said that the text is wrong. With this, Reuven explains his re-construction of the text, and how it fits perfectly with the simplest commentary. Quietly, Gershenson asks if Reuven did this on his own, and when he says yes, Gershenson says that Reuven's father is a good teacher. Gershenson tells Reuven that although he isn't opposed to such methods himself, Reuven must never use them in his class. Reuven agrees, and Gershenson says that he will call on Reuven often, now that they have this understanding. Gershenson dismisses Reuven with a smile.

This test of Reuven's intellect establishes him as an individual. Because of Reb's orders, Danny is by necessity part of the novel's background at this point, though he is the true main character; David also, by virtue of his poor health, is thrust off-stage, leaving Reuven with virtually no choice but to step up and forge an identity for himself, free from the influence and overshadowing of these two people in his life. He does so, as a person and a character, and as a result, those around him (and readers) come to admire him, making it apparent that like his father, he will contribute great things to his community, and do so by absorbing elements from different worlds and processing the best of each into a harmonious balance.

Later, Reuven goes to the library and looks up Rav Gershenson in the English and Hebrew catalogs, but finds his name nowhere; though the implication of this isn't wholly clear, the passage seems to hint that the rabbi is a Hasid, and suddenly, Reuven realizes why his father isn't teaching at Hirsch College.

David comes home from the hospital in mid-March, but he's confined to his bed (**Chapter Fifteen**). Talking and listening tire him, so Reuven spends little time with him during the first six weeks, but nonetheless, his father's presence in the apartment cheers Reuven. At school, he's called on regularly now in Gershenson's class, and though Danny's silence remains unbroken, Reuven has come to terms with it.

Hostilities in the Middle East escalate at this time, with Jews killing Arabs and Arabs killing Jews, and the British are often caught in the crossfire. The Zionist groups at Hirsch grow more active, and Reuven cuts afternoon classes one day to load trucks in Brooklyn with uniforms, helmets, and canteens for the Haganah in Palestine. This activity makes Reuven feel more directly involved in the fight, and soon, the Haganah occupy Tiberias, Haifa, and Safed, and they help the Irgun capture Jaffa.

David, meanwhile, slowly gets stronger, walking around the apartment, talking at length about Palestine. David tells Reuven that the night he had the attack, he'd been asked to go, as a delegate, to Palestine during the coming summer. Reuven asks why David didn't tell him before, and David says he didn't want to upset him. And though they don't talk of it again, Reuven knows his father thinks of it; ironically, David "had worked so hard for a Jewish state, and that very work now kept him from seeing it."

One Friday, in the second week of May, Reuven and David cry when Israel is officially recognized as a nation, but on the same day, Arab armies begin their threatened invasion. Iraqis, Egyptians, and Jordanians attack different parts of Israel, and there's much bloodshed. A rumor circulates around Hirsch that a recent graduate was killed in Jerusalem, and this turns out to be true. The student had graduated before Reuven had begun his study, but he'd been a well-liked mathematics student who'd gone to Hebrew University in Jerusalem to pursue a doctorate. (Clearly, Potok made the casualty a math student to bring the tragedy even closer to home for Reuven, his father, and Danny; the same fate could easily have fell to Reuven, and it still could in the future.) The student joined the Haganah, and while trying to get a convoy through to Jerusalem— perhaps including the truck Reuven helped to pack with supplies—he'd been killed. In the second week in June, when fighting in Israel ceased due to a United Nations truce, everyone in the school attended an assembly in the student's memory.

According to Reuven, Reb Saunders' anti-Zionist organization died that day, at least within the confines of the school. Never again did Reuven see their leaflets around Hirsch College, indicating that no matter how strong Reb's beliefs, he knew when to quit, and when to give up a hopeless cause. Though tyrannical, this demonstration of rationality on his part foreshadows the confrontation he must ultimately have with his son, another entity over which he has little to no control.

After final exams, Reuven learns that he's earned all A's, and in July, the doctor tells him that not only can his father go to the Peekskill cottage in August, but that he can go back to teaching in September. He does, and Reuven begins his third year of college, declaring philosophy as his major. After a few months, David gets involved in Zionist activities again and teaches an adult class one night a week.

Late that spring, while Reuven eats lunch at school, Danny comes to his table, smiles, and sits down, asking for help with a graph. Obviously, Reb has finally lifted the ban on his son, showing, once again, a sympathetic sense of reasonableness when the battle is lost.

In **Chapter Sixteen, a**fter two years of silence, the two greet each other and apologize, and Reuven admits that he really needed Danny when his father became sick. Reuven asks Danny how he tolerates the silence, saying that he would lose his mind. Danny says that he's learned to live with it, and when Reuven asks again why Reb maintains a silence with Danny, Danny confesses that he still doesn't know. He insists that Reb's a great man, though, and must have a good reason. Reuven disagrees, saying the silence is crazy and sadistic, and that he doesn't like Reb at all. Danny says he's entitled to his opinion, and they fall quiet. Reuven's reaction to this reconciliation, of course, is exactly what readers expect of a balanced, mature person, but Danny's is more difficult to process. Even though losing Reuven's friendship was a terrible cost, and possibly unnecessary, he defends and trusts his father and bears no anger. Indeed, with the exception of some sadness, Danny expresses no real emotion at all—a point that will become important at the novel's conclusion.

The two young men discuss Danny's falling weight and eye problems, and then they set to work on the graph. That night, Reuven tells his father, who nods. Because Israel has been established, he says, the Zionism debate is over. David asks about Danny, and Reuven says that he doesn't look well. David asks if Reb still maintains the silence with his son, and Reuven says yes. David says that a man has a right to raise his son in the way that he sees fit, but "what a price to pay for a soul." This is the first real clue for readers as to the purpose behind Reb's silence, and though Reuven asks his father to explain his words, David demurs.

Danny and Reuven assume their old habits immediately, meeting to go to and from school, and eating lunch together. In Gershenson's class, the two monopolize many class discussions, such that the rabbi must stop them in order to let others speak.

A few days into their renewed friendship, Danny tells Reuven that he's resigned himself to experimental psychology, and that he's even begun to enjoy it. He's adopted the lexicon, Reuven notices, and math rarely gives him trouble now. One day, during lunch, Danny tells Reuven about a conversation he had with Appleman, wherein the professor told him that in order to contribute to the field of psychology, Danny would have to use scientific method. Danny still appreciates Freud but finds him limited in scope. Danny wants to learn about perception and the process of learning, but he wants to work with people, not rats. To this end, Appleman suggests that Danny pursue a doctorate degree in clinical psychology, perhaps at Columbia. He's mentioned none of this to his father yet, though, and says that he won't until the day of his smicha, or rabbinic ordination, the following year. This increases the tension, naturally, in that readers know the confrontation between Danny and Reb, and thus the novel's resolution, is coming soon.

During another lunch, Danny asks Reuven what good his logic studies will be when he enters the rabbinate. Reuven says he studies a good deal of philosophy and theology, and that these might inform his work. Danny says that he thinks of theology and logic as being worlds apart, and Reuven says that he hopes to reconcile them. The two again express wonder at the irony of their diverging, chosen paths.

In June, Danny's sister marries, and Reuven, the only non-Hasid, attends. He's startled at the change in Reb: his black beard is turning gray, and he's aged much. Levi is a bit bigger, though still fragile-looking, and Danny's sister is beautiful. Her new husband looks severe, though, and Reuven decides that he doesn't like him.

After school ends, Reuven heads to Danny's house one day in July. Because Reuven spent Shabbat afternoons studying Talmud with his father, he hasn't spoken to Reb since Danny's sister's wedding, so Reuven had planned to go back when school ended for the year. On this day, Danny leads him down the third floor hallway, where black-caftaned men wait silently to meet with Reb. Many greet Danny, and one very old man reaches out to touch Danny on the arm. Reuven finds this kind of idolatry distasteful, but this disdain had begun to apply to Reb Saunders and all things Hasidic as well. Danny and Reuven wait until a man leaves Reb's study, and then they go in.

Reb says he's glad to see Danny and asks why they never see him on Shabbos afternoons. Reuven tells him that he studies Talmud with his father, and Reb, with a sigh, says that although he would like to talk more, many people are waiting to see him. He asks Reuven to come over one Shabbos afternoon, and Reuven agrees to try. Reb says nothing, however, about Zionism, nor about the silence he imposed on Reuven and Danny. This makes Reuven dislike Reb even more than before, and even though David has previously told Reuven that he is the conduit through which Reb communicates with Danny, Reuven fails to remember the importance of his role and stubbornly, out of bitterness and anger, doesn't see Reb again that month.

Danny and Reuven's last year of college begins in September, and one day, while sitting in the lunchroom, Reuven tells a mildly anti-Hasidic story, and Danny laughs (**Chapter Seventeen**). Thus enboldened, Reuven repeats something he heard a student say a few days before: "The tzaddik sits in absolute silence, saying nothing, and all his followers listen attentively." Danny's face goes blank, and Reuven mutters an apology. Danny relaxes again, though, and says that there's truth to the statement, and that silence is something one can listen to and learn from. This baffles Reuven, and Danny tries to explain, saying that you have to want to listen to it, and that he sometimes hears cries of pain from the world. Reuven, still not understanding, asks if Danny now talks with his father, and Danny shakes his head. Changing the subject, Reuven, who's begun dating regularly on Saturday nights, suggests that Danny should find a girl—"a wonderful tonic for a suffering soul." Danny explains that his wife has already been chosen for him, and that this fact makes it all the harder for him to break free from his inherited trap, because it's not just his family that's involved.

In the third week of October, Danny's brother, Levi, has his bar mitzvah early Monday morning. After the service and kiddush, Reb approaches Reuven and asks why he never comes over anymore, indirectly trying to command him to come. Reuven explains that he studies Talmud with his father, and

Reb nods and walks away, his frame in a slump. Levi, Reuven notes, is now tall and thin, but his continued fragility shows in his translucent skin and fierce eyes. He will always be dependent on pills, Reuven notes, but his eyes communicate the idea that he will hold on to life, no matter what pain ensues. And indeed, the day following his bar mitzvah, Levi becomes violently ill and is rushed to the hospital in an ambulance. As it pulls away from the Saunders' home, Danny calls Reuven to tell him, and Reuven notes the panic in his friend's voice.

David hears worry in Reuven's voice, too, and Reuven, after he gets off the phone, tells his father what's happened. Later, the two go into Reuven's room, and David asks his son why he's so upset by this news, especially since Levi has fallen ill before. Reuven explains Danny's plan to pursue a doctorate in psychology and to refuse the position of tzaddik, handing it off, instead, to Levi, thus maintaining the family dynasty. David asks how long Reuven has known of this, and he says that he learned of it while living at the Saunders' during the summer David was sick. The father is surprised that it has been so long, and that Reuven didn't tell him, but then he asks if Danny realizes how much pain this will cause Reb Saunders. Reuven says Danny's dreading the day that he tells him, but then David asks Reuven a question he hasn't considered: "Is Danny thinking to abandon his Judaism?"

David points out that Danny can't be a psychologist if he looks like a Hasid, and that he must carefully prepare what he says to Reb Saunders, as well as anticipate any questions his father might have. Danny, David explains, is like a prisoner focused on getting out of jail—that is, he's so focused on escape that he hasn't planned for or considered what awaits him outside. Next, David asks if the silence between Danny and Reb is still intact, and Reuven explains Danny's observations about being able to listen to silence. This upsets David more than anything. He mutters contemptuously about the Hasidim feeling that the burden of the world is on their shoulders alone, and then tells Reuven that silence is a way of bringing up children. He doesn't understand it himself, but it was practiced in Europe by some Hasidic families, and, he adds harshly, "There are better ways to teach a child compassion."

Though Reuven still doesn't understand, David doesn't wish to speak of it anymore. He makes Reuven promise to speak to Danny, then leaves the room. Reuven plans to raise the subject the next day, but Danny's so distraught over Levi that Reuven can't. According to doctors, something Levi ate had caused an imbalance, significantly, in his blood chemistry. They put him on new pills and keep him in the hospital to see how they work. Danny's shrouded in misery all week.

The next Wednesday, Levi's released from the hospital, but Danny's mother is now confined to her bed with high blood pressure—likely stemming from worry. Danny tells Reuven this news at lunch the following day, while also saying that he plans to write to Harvard, Berkeley, and Columbia and apply for a psychology fellowship. Reuven asks how long Danny can keep this secret and urges him to tell Reb. Danny says he doesn't want his father's explosions of fury, and that he's tired of hearing only silence or explosions from his father. Reuven tells him what his own father said about the situation, and though Danny's uncomfortable that Reuven has told someone else about his plan, Reuven presses the question about Danny remaining an Orthodox Jew. Though Danny has every intention of remaining Orthodox, he finally admits that to function in this new world, he knows that he must abandon the earlocks, caftan, cords, and beard of the Hasidim. On this topic, Edward A. Abramson wrote, "the fact that Danny must relinquish his Hasidic identity in order to take advantage of these possibilities also tells us something of the demands that America makes on those who would achieve their dreams there" (19).

Reuven asks about Reb seeing his (Danny's) mail from the universities, and Danny panics, realizing that he can't possibly intercept it. Reuven suggests that Danny should speak with David, so that night, Reuven and Danny approach him in his study. Danny confirms that the planned day for his confession is his ordination day, and that he intends to refuse to marry the girl to whom he's promised. David notes that Reb will have to explain the situation to the girl's parents, as well as his followers, which will be hard.

David next broaches the topic of silence, asking if Danny can hear silence (he nods), and whether he resents his father for this silence (he shakes his head). Because Danny admits that he doesn't understand the reasoning, however, David tells him that Reb will explain it to him and will want Danny to raise his own children in this way. Finally, with one last plea to consider the wording of his confession carefully, David, with Reuven, escorts Danny to the door, and the young man leaves. Reuven asks about hearing silence, but David says nothing and returns to his study, closing the door.

Danny receives sealed letters of acceptance from all three universities, the last coming in late January. He realizes that his father usually picks up the mail, and he's sure that he has seen the return addresses, so he starts to panic, asking, "What is he waiting for?"

After a few days, Danny tells Reuven that his sister's pregnant; the news had made his father smile and his mother cry with joy. Reuven asks if Reb gave any indication of knowing about Danny's plans, but Danny says no. Reb has not raised Levi and Danny's sister in silence, only Danny, and this causes Reuven to state again that he doesn't like Reb.

Days later, Danny tells Reuven that Reb asked why Reuven never comes over on Shabbat. Not only does Reuven study with his father, but he tells Danny he's not eager to see Reb, anyway. Danny tells Reuven that he's decided on Columbia, though, and Reuven says that he should just tell Reb and get it over with. At first, Reuven says Danny can live with the Malters, but then he remembers that Danny can't eat at his house. Danny says he could possibly live with his sister, but that he's deathly afraid.

A few days later, Danny says that his father asked yet again about Reuven coming over, and though Reuven promises to try to come, he doesn't, blinded with his own fury about Reb.

Weeks pass into spring, and Danny works on a large psychology project while Reuven prepares a long logic paper. The day before Passover, Danny tells Reuven once more that his father has asked after him and wants him to come on the first or second day of Passover. Again, Reuven halfheartedly promises to try, but when he tells David about Reb's request that night, David grows angry. He tells Reuven that when someone wishes to speak to you, you must let him. Reuven doesn't understand, saying he only studies Talmud when he's there, but as David presses him, he realizes that Reb needs him there to talk about Danny. David says Reuven will go on the first day of the holiday, and when Reuven wonders why Reb didn't just tell him, David says that Reb has been telling him, but Reuven wasn't listening. Reuven has failed to understand the non-verbal communication that has evolved between Danny and Reb.

Reuven calls Danny to tell him that he will come.

In **Chapter Eighteen**, Reuven makes his way to Danny's apartment on the first day of Passover. The synagogue there seems full of memories and echoes of spoken words to Reuven—it is a place that's consumed with the past—and he wonders what memories will wash over him in Reb's study. Reuven and Danny soon head up to the third floor together, and in the study, Reuven thinks that the only thing that has changed is Reb himself, who has aged considerably. The young men take seats on each side of him, and Reb closes the Talmud. He remarks on how Reuven has finally come, and how he is a man now, though he had been a boy when he first came. Danny is also a man, Reb notes, and then he asks what Reuven will do after graduation. Reuven explains that he has another year to study for his smicha, and that he will then enter the rabbinate. The statement seems to pain Reb for a moment, but then he says that Danny will receive his smicha in June, and his voice trails off.

After fidgeting, Reb continues, saying that at that time, the two young men will go different ways, a statement that makes Danny shudder. Reb says that he knows, and has known for a long time. Though Danny moans, Reb doesn't look at him throughout this exchange; instead, he talks to his son by focusing on Reuven. Reb says that a man is born with only a spark of goodness, which is God, and that this spark must be guarded, nurtured, and fanned. The shell, that is the rest of man, must not be allowed to choke the spark, and the shell can consist of a number of elements: indifference, laziness, brutality, genius, etc. Reb was blessed with a brilliant son, but cursed with the difficulty of raising him. He says that he saw Danny reading, devouring a story at the age of four and realized then that his son had no soul, only a mind. The story had been about one Jew's struggles to reach Eretz Yisroel before he died, but Danny had enjoyed the story because he realized the power of his mind, relating the story back to his father from memory. This made Reb cry to God; he wanted a son with compassion, a heart, a soul, righteousness, mercy, and the strength to suffer and carry pain. Reb stops here, trembling, and Reuven sees Danny crying, his glasses pushed up onto his forehead, his hand covering his eyes.

Reb goes on to explain that his brother was a person with a mind like Danny's, though he suffered from a disease that left his body wasted. Reb says,

> I was only a child when he left to study in Odessa, but I still remember what he was able to do with his mind. But it was a cold mind, Reuven, almost cruel, untouched by his soul. It was proud, haughty, impatient with less brilliant minds, grasping in its search for knowledge the way a conqueror grasps for power. It could not understand pain, it was indifferent to and impatient with suffering. It was even impatient with the illness of its own body. I never saw my brother again after he left for the yeshiva. He came under the influence of a great mathematician and taught in a university. He died in a gas chamber in Auschwitz. I learned of it four years ago. He was a Jew when he died, not an observer of the Commandments, but not a convert, thank God. I would like to believe that before he died he learned how much suffering there is in this world. I hope so. It will have redeemed his soul.

Reb says that in spite of the fact that Reuven is now a man, he will not wholly understand this until many more years pass.

Obviously, the message is really for Danny, but Reb continues to focus on Reuven.

Reb explains how his father would wake him in the middle of the night, when he was very young, and tell Reb harrowing stories about the destruction of Jerusalem and the sufferings of the Jews, and how he took Reb to the hospital to speak with poor beggars. Reb admits then that his own father only spoke to him when they studied together, to encourage Reb to look inside himself, find stores of strength, and be in company with his own soul. Others questioned Reb's father, but in his defense, he said that words play tricks and actually mask, rather than expose, what is in the heart. In order to feel the pain of others, Reb's father believed, one must feel pain himself, and this disarms one's pride, arrogance, and indifference to others. This was hard for Reb to understand, but he eventually did, he says, and his father later explained that a tzaddik, more than anyone else, must understand pain, since he must carry the pain of his followers on his shoulders and thus relieve them of their burden. Thus, although readers had been previously gotten hints about why Danny was being raised in silence, Reb, in this final chapter, gets to justify and explain his philosophy and intentions, which were good, contrary to appearances.

Reb says that he can see that Reuven doesn't understand, but that Danny does. Reb didn't want Danny to be like his brother. In his mind, it's better to have no son at all than a brilliant one with no soul. Thus, when Danny was four and showed this great intellectual potential, Reb pondered how to teach his son about pain without driving him away from the Torah. He realized that because they were no longer in Europe, but in America, he could not control opportunities from outside the community that would tempt Danny. Reb knew he couldn't stop his son from going to the world for more knowledge, but he wanted to make sure that Danny didn't abandon his religious faith, and that he had "the soul of a tzaddik no matter what he did with his life."

Reb stops speaking and cries, mentioning what a price he has had to pay. He loved talking to, and playing with, Danny as a boy, and it was from this foundation that Danny's love and admiration for his father took root. Once, Danny asked Reb why he no longer answered his questions, and Reb answered that Danny needed to look inside himself. On another occasion, Danny laughed at a man and called him an "ignoramus," and this angered Reb, who told him to consider life from this man's perspective, specifically the pain he likely feels regarding his ignorance. These responses bewildered Danny, who also started to have nightmares, but Reb feels as though the silence ultimately did teach Danny about suffering.

After a pause, Reb tells Reuven that he and his father were a God-sent blessing, sent to be listening ears, and watching eyes, for Danny when he first wished to rebel. Reb says that he looked at Reuven and David's souls, not their minds, and knew of Reuven's good soul when Danny first talked about wishing to be his friend. Reb knows that Reuven still thinks the silence imposed on Danny was too cruel, but Reb argues that Danny learned from it. Let him be a psychologist, Reb says; Danny will still be a sort of tzaddik to the world, albeit a much more secular version. Going silent, Reb looks at Danny, who's crying, eyes still hidden beneath a hand. Then Reb says Danny's name. He must say it a second time before Danny looks up. Reb asks whether Danny will shave his beard and earlocks, and Danny nods. Quietly, Reb asks if Danny will still observe the Commandments, and Danny nods again.

Reb asks Reuven's forgiveness for his anger regarding Zionism. Reb says that he found meaning in his brother's death—and that of six million others—in God's will, not the establishment of a Jewish state. His voice breaks while asking Reuven's forgiveness again, and then he asks his son for forgiveness and stands. Reb announces that it is the Festival of Freedom, that Danny is now free, and then Reb leaves the room to lie down. Danny cries, and though Reuven places a hand on his friend's shoulder to comfort him, he finds himself crying, too. Later, they walk through the streets together for hours without speaking.

When Reuven comes home, he tells David all that happened, David says, "A father has a right to raise his son in his own way, Reuven." He still says that he still doesn't care for it, but allows that it may be the only way to raise a tzaddik. Reuven remarks that he's glad he wasn't raised that way, and David reminds him that he, as a father who's not a tzaddik, had a choice.

During the first morning Shabbat service in June, Reb announces to his followers that Danny is leaving to study psychology. While this shocks the congregation, all of whom stare at Danny, Reb says he respects his son's soul and mind; when Danny relays this to Reuven later, he notes the order of these elements. Also, Reb tells the followers that Danny will remain an observer of the Commandments and will thus receive Reb's blessing. Though the followers seem shaken, they will not question Reb's judgment. Two days later, Reb breaks off Danny's marriage arrangements, and though the announcement makes news at Hirsch, the students, Hasid and non-Hasid alike, are so steeped in final exams that the announcement stops engendering discussion after only a few days. In June, both Reuven and Danny graduate summa cum laude.

In September, when Danny is about to move into a room near Columbia, he comes to the Malters' home to say goodbye. His beard and earlocks are gone, having the physical embodiment of his culture. David tells him that Columbia's not far, and that they'll see Danny on Shabbat. Reuven asks how Reb reacted to Danny's change in appearance. Danny says Reb didn't like it, but Danny also mentions that he and Reb speak now. David Malter asks Danny if he will raise his sons in silence. Danny says that he will if he can't find another way. David nods.

Reuven walks Danny down the street, and Danny asks if Reuven will come to study Talmud with him and Reb on some Shabbat afternoons. Reuven says, "Of course," and they shake hands. Reuven watches Danny walk away, his metal capped shoes tapping on the sidewalk, until he turns on Lee Avenue and disappears. As one critic noted, Danny's "'voyage' by subway to Columbia University is his voyage of discovery to his New World" (Sternlicht 47).

Abramson noted that one of the main criticisms of the novel

is the way "everything works out well for the protagonists, Potok being at base optimistic" (17). Nonetheless, scholar Sheldon Grebstein noted, "At the story's end the novel's two young heroes are about to realize the reward they have earned: a limitless future. In sum, *The Chosen* can be interpreted from this standpoint as an assertion of peculiarly American optimism and social idealism. Very simply, it says Yes" (25).

Works Cited

Abramson, Edward A. *Chaim Potok*. Boston: Twayne, 1986.

Bluefarb, Sam. "The Head, the Heart and the Conflict of Generations in Chaim Potok's *The Chosen*." *College Language Association Journal* June 1971, 402–9.

Grebstein, Sheldon. "The Phenomenon of the Really Jewish Bestseller: Potok's *The Chosen*." *Studies in American Jewish Literature* Spring 1975, 23–31.

Marovitz, Sanford. "Freedom, Faith, and Fanaticism: Cultural Conflict in the Novels of Chaim Potok." *Studies in American Jewish Literature* 4 (1986): 129–140.

Stampfer, Judah. "The Tension of Piety." *Judaism* Fall 1967, 494–98.

Sternlicht, Sanford. *Chaim Potok: A Critical Companion*. Westport, CN: Greenwood Press, 2000.

Walden, Daniel, editor. *Conversations with Chaim Potok*. Jackson: University of Mississippi Press, 2001.

Critical Views

EDWARD A. ABRAMSON ON POTOK'S DEPICTION
OF JEWISH AND NON-JEWISH WORLDS

The only non-Jewish characters who appear in the novel are patients or relatives in the Jewish hospital to which Reuven goes for treatment of his injured eye. The most thoroughly presented is Tony Savo, who occupies the bed next to Reuven. Potok presents him as a decent man who has no anti-Jewish prejudice and who illustrates in a minor way the importance of faith. He has been a boxer, and will lose his eye because of punches received in the ring. He sees Reuven eating while wearing a skullcap and comments on the importance of religion. Then he says, "Could've been on top if that guy hadn't clopped me with that right the way he did. Flattened me for a month. Manager lost faith. Lousy manager" (49). A page later he repeats the point about his manager losing faith. While this remark may be interpreted as the manager "losing faith" in Tony Savo, we learn that Tony wanted to be a priest once but chose the ring instead, a "Lousy choice," he now feels. As these points are made against the background of the radio's reports of the fighting toward the end of World War II, one feels the contrast between the violence in Europe and simple faith. It is a somewhat simplistic comparison but does highlight Potok's feeling that violence implies a lack of faith both in mankind and in something greater than man.

Danny arrives and tries to apologize to Reuven, who will not listen to him. Mr. Savo comments:

"He one of these real religious Jews?" Mr. Savo asked.
"Yes."
"I've seen them around. My manager has an uncle like that. Real religious guy. Fanatic. Never had anything to do with my manager though. Small loss. Some lousy manager." (67–68)

94

There is a dual implication here in that his manager's loss of faith is seen as being in some way responsible for Tony Savo's plight and the fact that his manager's religious uncle would have nothing to do with him is yet another sign of the manager's faithlessness. However, Danny and the uncle, religious though they are, are "cloppers": "You're a good kid. So I'm telling you, watch out for those fanatics. They're the worst cloppers around" (81). Religion is a good thing, but not the fanatical type of religion followed by the Hasidim; that is destructive. Thus, Potok uses a non-Jew to present the argument at the center of the religious confrontation which pervades the novel. Indeed, much later on when Reuven decides to become a rabbi, he remembers Tony Savo:

> "America needs rabbis," my father said.
> "Well, it's better than being a boxer," I told him.
> My father looked puzzled.
> "A bad joke," I said. (219)

The only other non-Jews who appear in the novel are Billy Merrit and, very briefly, his father. Billy's eye operation is unsuccessful, and he remains blind; Mr. Savo has to have one eye removed. Only Reuven completely heals. Indeed, good fortune will follow him throughout the novel, everything he puts his hand to reaching a satisfactory conclusion. It is one of the criticisms which has been leveled at the novel: everything works out well for the protagonists, Potok being at base highly optimistic, at least as far as his main characters are concerned. This issue will be pursued further later in this chapter.

The world outside the Hasidic community has a crucial effect upon Danny Saunders, the central figure in the plot. He tells Reuven that he feels "trapped" by the assumption that he will carry on the generations-old tradition that his family provides the rebbe for the community. He finds study of the Talmud extremely limiting and must sneak off to the public library and seclude himself behind the shelves in order to read books from the secular world. It is noteworthy that "misbehavior" in *The Chosen* consists of a genius reading the writings of some of the best minds of the last two centuries; one is not dealing here with Danny's reading pornography or popular culture. The nature of his reading highlights the repressiveness of the Hasidic world that his father rules.

(...)

Danny's attraction to psychology is an attraction to what has become almost a secular religion, with people like Sigmund Freud constituting members of a priestly caste. Not only does Danny discover that he can use the methods of Talmudic study in deciphering Freud's writings, but Reb Saunders finds that he can partially justify his son's choice of vocation in that Danny "will be a *tzaddik* for the world. And the world needs a *tzaddik*" (280). This explains Hugh Nissenson's remark that "Danny's conflict between the secular and the spiritual life has been daringly, and brilliantly resolved."9 One might also add, given Reb Saunders's perhaps somewhat too easy acceptance of his son's choice, that the conflict has been a bit too comfortably resolved.

Part of the reason for Danny's being drawn to the secular world lies in the comparative weakness of his Hasidic beliefs. Louis Jacobs states that while it is difficult to find a set of Hasidic doctrines that are acceptable to all Hasidic sects, there are "certain basic themes and a certain mood, founded on the pantheistic beliefs that are fairly constant. Among the ideas stressed in every variety of Hasidic thought are: the love and fear of God; *devekut*, 'cleaving' to God at all times; *simhah*, 'joy' in God's presence; *hitlahavut*, 'burning enthusiasm' in God's worship; and *shiflut*, 'lowliness,' 'humility,' construed as a complete lack of awareness of the self."10 It is noteworthy that Danny does not illustrate in his life any of these beliefs or actions. Indeed, his concerns are almost entirely with how he can achieve self-fulfillment and pursue the secular studies for which he has a growing passion. One critic has stated that "Danny", for want of a better word—the word has been overly used and abused, though it applies here—has been alienated— from his father, from Hasidism, and finally from the Hasidic community itself."11

Historical events thrust themselves with great force upon the characters. I have already discussed the reactions of Reb Saunders and David Malter to the Holocaust and the rebirth of Israel, events that Potok uses to show basic theological differences between the two men and the two religious groups. Potok also mentions the death of President Roosevelt and devotes most space to the Malters' reaction, with Reuven weeping and his father deeply grieved. They are placed within the context of the typical American reaction to the tragic event, as seen by descriptions of people stunned or crying in the street. Danny feels that the death is a "terrible thing," but we are not given Reb Saunders's reaction. This lack of information heightens the reader's sense of the Hasidic leader's apartness from secular, non-Jewish events. It may show some of Potok's bias in favor of David Malter, who has earlier told Reuven that he "should nor forget there is a world outside" (55).

(...)

Potok manages to permit the boys to remain strongly Jewish while taking advantage of the opportunities offered by American society. In this he differs from most other Jewish-American authors whose Jewish characters frequently must sacrifice important aspects of their Jewishness in order to take advantage of American opportunity. Indeed, the majority of the characters in twentieth-century Jewish-American writing do not view the relinquishment of their Jewishness as a major sacrifice. Describing a symposium held by the *Contemporary Jewish Record* (*Commentary*'s predecessor) in 1944 entitled "American Literature and the Younger Generation of American Jews," David Daiches observes that "Many of the contributors to the symposium seemed to think that their Americanism had subsumed their Judaism. One writer went so far as to equate the 'Declaration of Independence' with certain Jewish prayers, and Lincoln with Hillel."[13]

The enormous effect of the American Dream or, in Danny's case in particular, American opportunity as an inherent aspect of the Dream, is stated in part by Loren Baritz when he writes that the Jew had almost always "managed to resist the particular physical locale of his Galut by remembering his participation both in history and in the Jewish community. But because when we moved to America we responded to a psychological reversal promised by the American Dream—a promise of the end of Galut—we became more susceptible to the incursions of American utopianism, of America's rejection of the past, of age, and of continuity with Europe."[14] While Danny does not take his attraction to American opportunity so far as to reject the past, to reject Judaism, one can see in his rejection of his father's Hasidism an awareness that American society will permit both a secular profession and a Jewish life. However, even America makes demands of those who wish to use its gifts: Danny Saunders cannot retain his Hasidic way of life and his Hasidic appearance and still become a successful psychologist in America. As Baritz also writes: "Because of America's rejection of the past, of the fierce commitment to the notion that this land will start anew, the American Jew is pulled apart. To be a Jew is to remember. An American must forget."[15] Danny must "forget" some of his Hasidic ways.

(...)

Potok has reservations concerning the importance of the American Dream and American optimism in *The Chosen*. He asserts that "A covering hypothesis regarding the popularity of my work should take into account the many Jewish and non-Jewish readers of Potok ... in France, Germany, England, Holland, Japan, Australia, the Philippines, and elsewhere, including the Soviet Union. What do all those people know about Horatio Alger, ... American optimism and social idealism, and the American reverence for the pioneer?"[16] This comment appears in an essay in which Potok addresses himself to remarks made by Sheldon Grebstein a year earlier (see note 12). While one can sympathize with Potok's point to a degree, it remains true that with its American setting, the nature of Danny Saunders's belief in what is possible, Reuven Malter's basic faith that his future lies in his own hands, and the ultimate success of these characters and, indeed, of David Malter in achieving his goals, the novel exudes a type of optimism that is strongly associated with America. That this optimism and level of success can exist elsewhere is not in doubt; that it underlies, indeed pervades, *The Chosen* is what gives the book its American ethos. Non-Americans can appreciate and understand this ethos because of general cultural dissemination of American ideals and, not inconsiderably, because of the attitudes that Potok describes in the novel.

Notes

9. Hugh Nissenson, review of *The Chosen*, *New York Times Book Review*, 7 May 1967, 5.

10. Jacobs, *Hasidic Prayer*, 14.

11. Sam Bluefarb, "The Head, the Heart and the Conflict of Generations in Chaim Potok's *The Chosen*," *College Language Association Journal* 14 (June 1971): 405.

12. Sheldon Grebstein, "The Phenomenon of the Really Jewish Best Seller: Potok's *The Chosen*," *Studies in American Jewish Literature* 1 (Spring 1975): 25.

13. David Daiches, "Breakthrough," in *Contemporary American Jewish Literature: Critical Essays*, ed. Irving Malin (Bloomington, 1973), 31.

14. Loren Baritz, "A Jew's American Dilemma," *Commentary*, June 1962, 525.

15. Ibid.

16. "Reply to a Semi-Sympathetic Critic," 31.

LESLIE FIELD ON POTOK'S "DIFFERENCE" FROM OTHER JEWISH WRITERS

When Chaim Potok published his first novel, a colleague said: "He's not like the other Jewish-American novelists being read by the general American public. He's an entirely new breed. The critics won't know what to do with him." Potok has written five novels over a period of fifteen years and it would now seem propitious to take stock. What have the critics been saying during these years?

Potok burst upon the Jewish-American fiction scene in 1967 with the publication of *The Chosen*. Immediately he was hailed as a "different" kind of writer. Up to that time the "Hart-Schaffner-Marx" of Jewish-American fiction had been Bellow-Malamud-Roth (Philip). All three wryly joked about the clothing industry label with which they had been tagged by critics. But they really detested it. They wanted to be known simply as American writers who "happened to be" Jewish, not some hybrid, hyphenated brand of writer, certainly not Jewish-American. They have been vociferous in their condemnation of what they consider reductive schematization. Generally, they believed Jewish-American a slight niche in the scheme of literature, which insensitive critics had slipped them into, and they wanted no part of it, or almost no part. When it suited their purposes they would initiate discussions of their Jewish backgrounds and the Jewish milieus of their writing.

Critics too wrestled with the Jewishness of the three writers. They were considered marginal Jews, ambivalent Jews, self-conscious Jews, timid Jews, to list some of the milder epithets. But for Potok these terms were inapplicable. He was, indeed, a new kind of popular Jewish writer.

A few years ago Daphne Merkin summed up the difference nicely: "After all the countless portrayals in American fiction of wandering and assimilated Jews—from Malamud's S. Levin to Bellow's Moses Herzog to Roth's Alexander Portnoy—the literary public, at least a large and enthusiastic segment of it, would seem to be ready for Chaim Potok's version of the American Jew—one who has never left the traditional Jewish community."[1] She went on to say that "unlike more consequential Jewish writers whose heritage colors but does not dictate to their material, Potok writes both *as* a Jew and *because* he is a Jew."[2] Ignore for the moment her use of "consequential," and she has undoubtedly provided a workable coup de grâce for Potok classification.

Notes

1. Daphne Merkin, "Why Potok is Popular," *Commentary* 61 (February 1976), p. 73.

2. Merkin, p. 74.

SHELDON GREBSTEIN ON THE REASONS FOR THE NOVEL'S POPULARITY

Or, to reach a little further back in time, what would seem an unlikelier best-seller than a first novel by an unknown writer with an unpronounceable name, a novel about orthodox Jews, especially Hasidic Jews, set in the Brooklyn of the early 40s, and a novel whose most stirring action is a schoolboy softball game? Yet Chaim Potok's novel *The Chosen*, which is my main concern in this paper, was a best-seller indeed, even rising to the exalted number-one position on the *New York Times* list. It is a book totally devoid of such sure-fire elements as violence, sexuality or romantic love. Its setting is wholly mundane. Its cast of characters derives from groups whose activities can hardly be said to grip the American imagination. It recounts no valiant deeds. It devotes many pages to such uncaptivating subjects as Biblical exegesis and the history of Hasidism. Its style ranges from undistinguished to banal. Its tone is subdued and utterly humorless. Its pace is moderate. Its overall color is gray. With all these handicaps, that *The Chosen*—this really Jewish book—should have attained best-sellerdom seems more than a phenomenon; it is truly a miracle.

But miracle or not, its 38 weeks on the list is an obdurate fact demanding explanation. Although best-sellers cannot be predicted—for if we knew the secret in advance, would we not all be rich and famous novelists?—they can always be explained after the fact. Pragmatically such analysis is irrelevant in that it has little effect upon the creation of new best-sellers, but it is nevertheless an alluring sort of inquiry for what it tells us about a particular moment in our culture and about the audience response to narrative. In other words, the investigation of popular novels, quite aside from the question of artistic quality, a question I will consider later in the paper, can produce a clearer understanding of why and how we read, and of the reasons for our choices of what we read.

To be specific, what elements in *The Chosen*, in our time, and in ourselves brought this unlikely candidate for success to a position of such prominence?

(...)

Indeed, *The Chosen* exemplifies some of the basic emphases and materials of the Jewish Movement: moral fervor, strong emotions experienced by sensitive characters, the portrayal of ancient and deeply-felt traditions, the depiction of intimate family life, and an essentially affirmative view of human nature. Moreover, all this is enhanced by the circumstances of an alien and thus intriguing life-style.

Yet with all these Jewish traits, the novel is also specifically American. And here we must remind ourselves that the appeal of popular literature shares in the appeal inherent in all art— the power to render archetypal experience in accessible cultural forms, albeit in popular literature the power is of a different order of intensity and profundity. Accordingly, the American cultural myth or fable at the heart of *The Chosen* is essentially that of both of the Horatio Alger stories and *The Great Gatsby*—the dream of success. In this version the story is played out by an improbable but possible "only in America" cast of Hasidic and orthodox Jews, who demonstrate that people can still make good through hard work, and that severe difficulties can be overcome by pluck, integrity, and dedication. At the story's end the novel's two young heroes are about to realize the reward they have earned: a limitless future. In sum, *The Chosen* can be interpreted from this standpoint as an assertion of peculiarly American optimism and social idealism. Very simply, it says Yes.

Another element irresistibly attractive to the American audience is the novel's nostalgia. It combines a return to the inspiring days of World War II, in our imagination a clean and just war which we won completely over formidable enemies who had attacked *us*, with the evocation of some enduring institutions as the nuclear family, comradeship, and that old-time religion. In these respects the novel offered its troubled readers a stay against the confusion and crises of the '60s: the disintegration of the family, the Vietnam conflict, the campus rebellion.

Concomitantly, the novel is centrally concerned with the conflict between parents and children integral to all these events, but, unlike what happened all too often in reality, it allows the young to gain maturity, personal fulfillment and freedom in abundant measure, yet not over their parents' dead bodies. In the battle between Reb Saunders and Danny, a special case of the eternal combat between the old and the new, wounds are inflicted on both sides. But they heal, and all are a little stronger for it. In accordance with our cultural myth, the novel's real heroes are its young, champions of the New. Nevertheless, the parents' role has also been reaffirmed. As Granville Hicks pointed out in the *Saturday Review*, good fathers and good sons are rare figures in contemporary American fiction. Although the fathers and sons here are not "pals," they are motivated by love and mutual respect.

There is even an appeal to the American reverence for the pioneer. In this version the tale deals not with the physical exploration and conquest of the wilderness, but the plunge into the cultural and intellectual unknown by immigrant groups. *The Chosen* focuses not on the newcomers' first encounter with the material conditions of the new world, but that exciting second phase of assimilation in which the host culture is enriched by the absorption of the best members and qualities of the sub-cultures, while they themselves still retain their character and individuality.

(...)

This second antithesis, reason versus faith, is really a simplistic summary of a complex process. The very method or style of each team's play is significant. Reuven's team operates by skill, practice, training, logic; Danny's by sheer energy, concentration, dedication. The game escalates into a holy war because the Hasidic team perceives their opponents as *apikorsim*—Jews who have abandoned and desecrated the faith. The same opposition and tension persists into the relationship of the two boys and the inter-relationships of fathers and sons. Moreover, it defines the very process of growth or maturity each boy experiences. Reuven represents the logical, inductive, and quantitative: Danny the intuitive, deductive, qualitative. To be complete Reuven must learn the power of faith, the unquestioning devotion to a principle; on the other side, Danny must expand his vision and learn to think rationally and objectively. Indeed, Danny's growth and break to freedom can be described as his successful adaptation to the scientific method. He can go on to advanced study in psychology—the probing into the mysteries of human behavior—only after he has mastered mathematics. As the other half of the paradox or reversal, Reuven gifted in math, is moved to enter rabbinical training.

(...)

Seeing versus blindness and talk versus silence are two other recurrent patterns in the novel. Reuven begins to see when his glasses are broken and his eye injured. In other words, this is a paradigm for sight and insight, and yet another version of the outer/inner or material/spiritual antithesis. Similarly, talk and silence function in an inverse or paradoxical way. Although important truths are conveyed in speech, many others are communicated by silence. Reuven, for example, who is not being raised in the method of silence, learns much from his father on those occasions when his father should speak but does not. Again à la Hemingway, Mr. Malter has a habit of "looking" at Reuven or of deliberately maintaining silence as a mode of response to Reuven's hasty, superficial or erroneous judgments. Eventually Reuven catches on and begins to speak with consistent wisdom.

The major component of the health/sickness contrast is the constant reminder of Mr. Malter's fragility of physical health, his recurrent bouts of illness, juxtaposed against his intellectual strength and moral stamina. This characterization—with the hovering possibility always in the readers consciousness that he may die—represents the situation of Judaism as Potok implies it. That connection is re-enforced in the novel's last third by a number of passages which place in close proximity mentions of his delicacy or sickness with references to the Holocaust, the struggle to establish Israel, and the controversies among Jews over both these events. For example, at the end of Chapter Eleven Mr. Malter declares: "The Jewish world has changed.... A madman has destroyed our treasures. If we do not rebuild Jewry in America, we will die as a people." Immediately thereafter we are informed that he suffers a near-fatal heart attack. However, like both American Jewry and Israel, he survives, and at the end of the novel he is well again.

SANFORD E. MAROVITZ ON THE ROLE OF RELIGIOUS FAITH

It has often been charged that Potok's fiction is all of a kind, and in a limited way that is true, but the structural and thematic correspondences are by no means tiresomely repetitive, and they do not diminish the attractiveness of the narratives or the drama with which he presents his confrontations among ideas and characters. Potok is a highly learned and intellectual writer, a novelist of ideas. An ordained rabbi with a doctorate in philosophy, he wanted to be an artist and a storyteller since his school days, but he had no intention even as a young man of becoming simply an entertainer with his fiction. Instead he expected readers to learn from it. Not that he wished to be didactic in the hard sense, hammering in lessons as if with a mallet of absolute truth, but to convey through the representation of manifold possibilities, how one might live a rich, meaningful, and worthwhile life in the midst of a largely secular culture characterized by egocentricity, materialistic values, the compulsive demand for novelty, a dearth of spiritual vitality, and—as Saul Bellow has often said—

apparently endless distraction.[4] This is the culture that Potok calls "western secular humanism," the culture that holds out, as if with open hands, a multitude of temptations to draw the young Jewish heroes of his first five novels farther and farther from the traditional community of faith in which they were reared and which struggles, at times fiercely, to keep them in the fold.

It must be understood, however, that these temptations are no mere tinsel lures offering momentary or material pleasures, but are far more compelling ones than those to an intellectual youth burning to learn all that he can, however he can—through science, analysis, and rational inquiry. If Potok's young protagonists are all Jewish, their struggle to break away from the traditions that bind them—but without simultaneously alienating themselves from the family, the community, and the faith that has nurtured them (again with the exception of Davita)—should not be seen as a narrow provincial tale of New York Jews, Hasidic or otherwise. Instead, they reflect the author's own ability to fuse his Hebrew learning and faith with the most worthy features of secular humanism into a kind of spiritual-intellectual bridge and mediate between them, a quality of mind that has led Daniel Walden to describe Potok as a "*Zwischenmensch*," a "between-person."[5] Potok calls the "mechanism" for this fusion, "a selective affinity."[6]

(...)

Tracing the responses of Potok's young protagonists to the threats and temptations of secular America in contrast to the security offered by their nuclear communities of faith illuminates an essential purpose in his writing. He believes that there is a need of and a place for faith in the contemporary world and that it does not have to be compromised in order to remain viable. He shows, however, that faith is something to be understood as well as accepted and that such an understanding cannot be achieved without confrontation, struggle, and pain. Nor can it be either acquired or sustained by ignoring the additions to knowledge that are a part of the modern world.

But once this understanding has been achieved, Potok suggests, and he certainly does not mean for Jews alone, it constitutes with the faith itself a vital moral and spiritual source from which one may continuously draw toward filling his brief span of life with meaning.

Notes

4. See, for example, Saul Bellow, "The Individual in an Ocean of Noise," *Akron Beacon-Journal*, 4 Feb. 1973, Sec. E, p. 4. Extracts are published from a lecture at the Smithsonian Institution delivered by Bellow earlier in the same year.

5. Daniel Walden, "Chaim Potok, A Zwischenmensch ('between-person') Adrift in the Cultures," *Studies in American Jewish Literature*, 4 (1985), 19–25.

6. Quoted by S. Lillian Kremer, "An Interview with Chaim Potok, July 21, 1981," *Studies in American Jewish Literature*, 4 (1985), 85.

JUDAH STAMPFER ON POTOK'S MISREPRESENTATIONS OF HASIDIC LIFE

The Chosen is a first novel, not the settled expression of a veteran novelist; though its author has written many short stories. Its strengths and weaknesses are quickly apparent. Its opening scene, of the ball game where Danny Saunders hits Reuven Malter in the eye with a pitched ball and almost blinds him, has a high cadence, the smack of action, and an overtone of mythic bravura. No episode later in the novel comes up to this one in excitement, though other values emerge. Potok is a veteran short-story writer. He can sweep in a high-keyed scene.

In its plot, the novel is the story of Danny Saunders, his training to be a Hasidic *rebbe*, and his abandonment of it for a career in psychology. The choice is crystal-clear; so is its resolution. The characters come in heavy outline, in their stations in life, the positions they adopt vis-à-vis each other. They are hieratic. With more mellow experience in writing, Potok may introduce more spontaneous conversation, a few lyric moments, some unexpected reversals and complexities of character. Here, the movement of the story is king.

(...)

Its description of American Hasidic life, as I have known it, has only the most superficial resemblance to its outer behavior. As appreciative as Potok is of the Jewish community, even he cannot escape the bent of Anglo-Jewish novelists, to write of aspects of Jewish life of which they are not deeply acquainted and make them seem darker, more rigid, and more unattractive than they really are.

Let me be specific. Danny's father trains his son by debating Talmudic problems with him in public on the Sabbath. I have never seen this happen among Hasidim; they bandied words of wisdom, stories, and sermonettes, but it could conceivably happen in a strong Yeshiva atmosphere. But the father deliberately makes mistakes for his son to catch. Such a gesture no Hasidic *rebbe* would ever do before his congregation. A holy man, a voice of God's truth, does not engage in such devious gestures in public. It rings tricky, and goes against the whole grain of the institution. In fact, the entire obsession with learning was not appropriate to these Hasidim. The *rebbe*, Reb Saunders, preaches a lengthy sermon to his congregation on the importance of Torah study. This might be appropriate in a Yeshiva. To a Hasidic congregation, it is like preaching diagnostic technique or surgical procedure to a drugstore salesman. The *rebbe* would preach holiness, *mitzvot*, love, faith, the Sabbath, but not close and careful study of texts. In fact, Reb Saunders' entire course of study was that of a teacher in a Yeshiva. No Hasidic *rebbe* I knew studied the Talmud with his dedication. They were learned men, but studied mystical tracts and Hasidic material.

Nor were the American Hasidic dynasties this tightly dynastic. *The Chosen* has almost no women in it. It is a man's book. Danny's sister appears briefly and sketchily, and comes to marriage in docile acquiescence to her father's decision. In actuality, the daughters of these Hasidic *rebbes* were fascinating and complex women; father or no, they had to be wooed by the man, however briefly, to be won by him. I recall one *rebbe*'s daughter who ran away from home for half a year on an arranged marriage, and had to be courted gallantly by her bearded betrothed. In an even more extreme case that became a legend, a girl went through the wedding ceremony, then, late that night in her bridal room—so the story went—told her husband, "My father could make me take your ring, my father could make me sip your wine; but my father can't make me get into that bed with you." The marriage was quickly annulled. And even when fulfilled in love, the marriage has a lively, as well as a dynastic, flavor. It was never, to my memory, this mildly acquiescent, without the vitality of lived experience.

The Hasidic dynasties were, God knows, fanatic enough, but not so fanatic (at least then in America) that they would be literally out for Jewish blood; yet Danny bats for the pitcher's head, as he says flatly:

> "Your father is David Malter, the one who writes articles on the Talmud?"
> "Yes."
> "I told my team we're going to kill you apikorsim this afternoon." He said it flatly, without a trace of expression in his voice.

This is, at least, *retzichah beshogeg*, homicide, if not *bemezid*, premeditated murder. Murder is murder. If Danny meant it, and the book delivers it straight, then the book does not handle its psychology with complete respect. Emotionally, Danny is loaded not with frustrated ambition, but murderous hate. In the story, the impulse is dropped with simple regret; but the impulse to murder requires a more drastic catharsis. And in any case, Hasidim, at least in America at that time, were not that lethal. I remember a particular instance, strikingly parallel to this one, when such a Hasidic crown prince came to a baseball game, not to play, but to recite Psalms for his team's victory. When they did badly, he simply raised his voice. As I recall, the technique worked. His team won, no blood, no hate, just a funny way to win at baseball.

Even the central crisis of the book, Danny's heritage of the mantle of *rebbe* when he wanted to be a psychologist, was not strictly a matter of primogeniture, but decided in each case afresh, with great personal attunement to the man involved, not as an automatic inheritance as on page 112. The instant one reads that Danny had a younger brother, one wonders what the tension is all about. Danny should get it. If he doesn't want it, or isn't worthy, then let his brother get it, or even his future brother-in-law. This, in fact, is the resolution of the book; but it was no great stumbling block to begin with. Here, also, the author makes Hasidic life rigid, dynastic, and inflexible in a way that loses its vivacious flavor.

(...)

Read as a conflict between the Hasid and the Misnagdim, the book is too freighted with anti-Hasidic prejudice to be of value. For reasons like those given above, this was not their style of life. But Potok's depiction of Yeshiva life has a ring of truth. The book should then be read as a book about the conflict between true piety and blind fanaticism, with the Hasidic element an emblem of the fanatic. And here, too, the book touches a deep social chord. Potok is an ordained rabbi. His stories, his sermons, have a learned and reverent ring. More than literary interest is involved in such a man's tale of how religious fanaticism can be mellowed into a more humanistic piety.

SANFORD STERNLICHT ON POTOK'S SYMBOLISM

The description of the world of New York City Hasidism is fascinating to the reading public, both Gentile and Jewish. Potok has excellent descriptive powers, and his portrayal of the seemingly exotic community and its environs is like a travelogue to a foreign land inhabited by a very different people. This is not only the experience of the reader; it is the same for the point-of-view character/narrator, Reuven. The accuracy, detail, and richness of Potok's re-creation of a specific community at a certain time is one of the major achievements of *The Chosen*. One could also compare aspects of the novel to a documentary film depicting a society radically different from mainstream America. A camera eye seems to roam the streets and enter into homes and the synagogue with Reuven. The documentary quality is emphasized by the frequent interjections of background "essays" on the historical evolution as well as the customs of the Hasidic community.

Potok's decision to use a first-person narrative for the telling of the story works particularly well. Reuven is appealing as a personality, and he is easy to identify with for young people. This technique fits very well with Potok's role as teacher/writer as does his use of interspersed documentation in the form of history or sociology lectures. The latter, for some readers, however, may prove to be somewhat off-putting or delaying of the narrative flow. Nevertheless, the serious reader should slow down and absorb the lessons. There is much to be learned from Chaim Potok.

Special note must be made of Potok's brilliant use of eye imagery in the novel. Eye/eyes/eyeglasses stand for seeing, opening up of vision, recognition, and so on. At the beginning of the novel, as the ball game has commenced, Reuven keeps pushing up his glasses on the bridge of his nose so that they won't fall off during an important play (15). This description establishes Reuven as a serious student, a reader, but also it foreshadows the accident to his eye that will happen shortly when it is struck by a piece of eyeglass. Glasses are both a way of seeing better and a barrier to the world. The glasses are broken. The sliver that enters his eye symbolically opens his eyes to the Hasidic world of his friend-to-be.

Danny's repentant visit to Reuven in the hospital is the beginning not only of friendship but also of Reuven's comprehension of the traditions and values of the Hasidic community that he and his friends have disparaged. Also, the suffering that Reuven endures because of his eye injury makes him more understanding of the suffering of others, starting with fellow patients on the eye ward of the hospital. It is a maturing factor. Reuven is very aware, as his eye slowly heals, of darkness and light, as when he leaves his father's dark study and enters the bright living room (100–102). When Danny is learning about earlier Jewish history, he recognizes that people are complicated because they are blind to themselves; that is, they lack insight (156).

As Danny comes to "see" more and more of the outside world his eyes begin to blink and tire (182, 184). Finally, as the young men have matured to their full height and have begun to grow facial hair, Danny is wearing glasses (203). Discovering the secular world that he finds so fascinating now requires the assistance of another set of eyes so to speak. This is surely an experience many young people have as they attack the mountains of printed material or Web sites they have been attracted to or required to read.

But eyes have other functions besides seeing. When Danny is forbidden to speak to Reuven, they communicate with their eyes (252). The final eye reference in the novel is on the last page when Danny's eyes glow as he realizes that he soon will be studying at Columbia University where there will be so much more of the world to "see" (284).

David L. Vanderwerken on the Function of Sports in Potok's Work

Everyone knows the softball game opening in Potok's 1967 *The Chosen*, where two yeshivas compete, with World War II providing a weighty backdrop. For these Jewish lads, Reuven Malter tells us, playing baseball is an "unquestioned mark of one's Americanism" (12), yet despite the warlike language of Coach Galanter, Reuven's team takes a fairly relaxed approach to the sport. Reuven's assimilationist Orthodox school team learns quickly that Danny Saunders and his separatist Hasidic forces are on hand to play hardball, treating this pastime as a kind of intramural Holy War against the non-Hasidic "apikorsim" (23), heretics who might as well be goyim. And we recall Danny's hardnosed play sends Reuven to the hospital with eye damage when Danny lines a shot off pitcher Reuven's face. Predictably, this inauspicious episode leads to a lasting friendship covering two novels worth, *The Chosen* and the 1969 sequel, *The Promise*. But you're probably hard-pressed to dredge up any other sporting motif or reference outside of this game in *The Chosen* that Potok uses as a cultural bridge to gently introduce goyische readers into the curious milieu of the Hasidim. However, the bulk of Potok's canon seems to be devoid of the play spirit. Indeed, baseball, or any other sporting activity, disappears from *The Chosen* after that apparently one-game season. Yet, upon closer inspection, sports, like human sexuality and humor, do form part of his invented world, although most critics would find the concepts of a "playful Potok," a "libidinous Potok," or a "comic Potok" oxymoronic.

In my 28 April 2000 interview with Potok, I asked him what role, if any, had sports played in his life and career. He replied, "I loved play and sports: Ringalevio, stickball, sandlot baseball. I played all the time. Then I started high school and I had less time for sports. But up until college, I loved sports. And then in the summer, when we were at camp, I loved tennis, rowing, I fished. Those were glorious years. And then came the seminary and instead of fishing, I worked" (Potok). Although he speaks in the past tense here, Potok allows that he does follow baseball and keeps up with Philadelphia's sporting scene. Clearly, though, Potok views play, game, and sport as exclusively the province of childhood and adolescence, not worthy of serious attention for adults.

Although Potok does not share the ultra-Orthodox position stated in *The Chosen*, that the yeshiva rabbis see sports as an "evil waste of time" (12) stolen from the study of Torah and Talmud, he generally adheres to the notion that mature people actualize themselves through work, not play.

In *My Name Is Asher Lev*, six-year-old Asher asks father Aryeh what section of the *New York Times* he is discarding:

"Sports," he said.

"You don't read sports, Papa?"

"It's a foolish waste of precious time," he said. Then he added in Yiddish, "It comes from the Other Side, Asher. Boxing, football.... People are hurt. It must come from the Other Side." (156)

Aryeh Lev articulates the ultra-Orthodox position succinctly enough. Sport is hurtful—physically, intellectually, and spiritually. Witness in *The Chosen* Reuven Malter's eye injury, and that of punchy boxer Tony Savo, Reuven's hospital mate; whose signature line is "cockeyed world" (57).

DANIEL WALDEN ON THE ROLE OF THEOLOGY IN POTOK'S WORK

More than any other art form, Potok wrote in explanation of the hero and the heroic ideal, "the novel has served to reflect the breakup of the old order of things, often at the cost of committing the fallacy of imitation." The novel has drawn for us a new model of reality. Indeed, the biblical heroes, he believes, were not detached and sublime members of a ruling class; they came from the people, they interacted with the people. Thus in his own world, study and faith and a coming to terms with other cultures were the normal enterprises of life, as they had been in the Jewish experience for at least two thousand years; it is the nexus where a certain binocular vision of reality fused all activity into a meaningful unity. "The heroes of my writing," Potok concluded, "are the action aspect of that vision of things; they are the ordinary people of my own private and precious world."[7] In turn, confronted with the choice of having to alter some of the basic assumptions of fundamental Judaism, or of rejecting the new model out of hand, he chose the former. He has chosen to resolve his problems by the use of modern historiography and the scientific approach to Judaism's sacred texts; as a result he sees only one world, one organic interweaving of the totality of the human experience. He decided to forge a religious life out of what he calls "provisional absolutes." Above all, there are two characteristics in common in these definitions of interpretation: "commitment to a value-charged universe that is intrinsically meaningful, and the assumed need for a pattern of significant activity that can concretize and infuse it into the everyday activities of man." Thus, perhaps tautologically, "The notion that the universe is intrinsically meaningful is for me a provisional absolute." Very simply, theology and behavior are organically related. A theology that is not related to a pattern of behavior is trivial. "And a pattern of behavior that is not linked to a system of thought is an instance of religious robotry."[8]

True, Sidney Hook argued, man may do it alone; but Potok added, provided he has faith in the tenet that he can do it alone. Hook as a naturalist, says Potok, denies the existence of the religious quest and thus is seen by the religionist as a blind man who denies the existence of color. "And that is why the religionist will deny that man can do it alone, for in point of fact man has never felt he can do very much alone without appealing to some such metaphysical entity as Math-Points, Atoms, Ideas, Universals, Forms, Universal movers, Substances, Logos, Reason, Nature, Natural Law, Conscience, Mind, Atomic Facts, Scientific Method, Immutable Logic, or, for that matter, the Nature of Man."[9]

No wonder Chaim Potok returned wistfully but realistically to the Bronx street he knew so well. Now a black neighborhood, the block had been the home of Italians and Jews who were somehow surviving the Depression and raising their children. Nearby was the Yeshiva where he'd studied for seven years; now it was a black Baptist Church. He remembered the little cap games that were played in his hallway. He recalled the time he'd lost his temper and shouted at a little black boy who was playing with three whites. He'd picked on him because he didn't live in the building, appeared the least capable and seemed an intruder. Only later, facing his father, did Chaim realize what he'd done. "I *saw* the words I had used and they were *alive*." It was after the event that his father asked for what reason had he used such words? Because the boy was different? Well, Tante Sarah and Yankele Rosenthal and Cousin Reuven were different. "How could we cry out when others used such words against us," his father queried, "if *we* used such words against other people who were born black?" The lesson was learned. The problem, Potok realized, was his, not the black boy's. Unfortunately, the category of color was a "bog," an impasse. "I am too much an American, and my Bronx street was a portrait painted in poisoned oiles."[10]

Notes

7. Chaim Potok, in *The Great Ideas Today* (Chicago: Encyclopedia Brittannica, 1973), p. 74.

8. "Chaim Potok's Answers to Five Questions," in *The Condition of Jewish Belief: A Symposium* (New York: Macmillan, 1966), pp. 171–179.

9. Chaim Potok, "The Naturalism of Sidney Hook," *Conservative Judaism* 18 (Winter 1964), pp. 40–52.

10. Chaim Potok, "Reflections on a Bronx Street," *The Reconstructionist* 30 (October 30, 1964), pp. 17–20.

DANIEL WALDEN ON POTOK'S FORMATION AS AN ARTIST

When he was sixteen, he read his first serious adult novel, Evelyn Waugh's *Brideshead Revisited*. Its effects were so vivid that Potok reveals its impact on him with incredible detail in nearly every interview presented here. "It absolutely changed my life," Potok explains. "I lived inside that book with more intensity than I lived inside my own world.... When I closed the book, I was *overwhelmed* by my relationship to that book. I remember asking myself, 'What did he do to me? How do you do this kind of thing with words?'" Soon after, Potok was deeply affected by another novel—James Joyce's *Portrait of the Artist as a Young Man*—and made a commitment to write. This decision was met with hostility among members of his former Hassidic community, prompting his move to the more liberal

Conservative branch of Judaism. This shift to writing and Conservative Judaism and his engagement with the Western world forced Potok to rebuild his world. When he decided to separate from the Hasidic community, he comments that "it wrenched my world entirely. I lost all of my friends. I lost most of my teachers. I had to literally reconstruct my existence."

The conflicts between Orthodox Jewish values with the world of Western secular humanism became central to Potok's work from then on, permeating his literature in what he continually calls a "core-to-core cultural confrontation." Nearly all of the sixteen interviews here feature Potok's reflections on the Western tradition of creating art—of which he is an active participant—and his heritage among people who are often suspicious of artistic endeavors and flights of imagination. Each of his novels have protagonists from the center of Jewish tradition, who are forced to confront and negotiate space with a crucial tenet of Western culture, be it Freudian psychoanalytical theory, text criticism or, most importantly, art.

Whether writing fiction, children's books, or popular histories such as *Wanderings: Chaim Potok's History of the Jews* (1978), Potok tracks the points in which secular culture collides and sometimes fuses with religious faith, in ways that are accessible to Jews and non-Jews alike. This aspect of his literature stems from both his experiences as a painter and his immersion into Western literature.

(...)

In addition to reading *Brideshead Revisited* and studying art such as Pablo Picasso's *Guernica*, a painting he emphasizes had a profound influence on his literature, Potok's life and art were also altered by his stint as an army chaplain during the Korean War. "It was for me, as an individual and a writer, the pivotal experience and remains the lynch pin in everything that has occurred to me in my life," he tells S. Lillian Kremer in 1981. "I went into that world one individual and came out another individual altogether." For the first time, he saw a pagan world that had not been affected by Judaism, and in which non-Jews worshipped and observed as intensely as he had. In several later interviews, he discusses the effect those two years had on his novels, especially *The Book of Lights*.

Whether the subject is his literature, his religious and academic scholarship, or his life, a conversation with Chaim Potok always seems to lead back to cultural conflicts and uneasy fusions. He sees all great art as something that emerges from the tensions between faith and culture, between the individual's beliefs and the cultural systems and ideas that permeate the artist's existence.

(...)

It's perhaps surprising that, considering the erudite and learned nature of these interviews, Potok's novels are generally quite appreciated and accessible. *The Chosen* was popular enough to be adapted into a film in 1980, and it—as are several of his works—is often assigned to high school students for class reading. The author freely discusses the hard work that goes into his attempts to make his writing as simple, but also as precise, as possible. His writing style is sometimes as intentionally unsophisticated and straightforward as his conversational style is elegant and complex.

Potok's contribution to literature is profound. It introduces the Western world to modern Orthodox Jewish communities, but perhaps more significantly it makes that very particular world seem eerily familiar to non-Jews. Though his novels are rooted in the past, in the era of his own childhood and adolescence, Chaim Potok as a conversationalist is deeply committed to the tensions of the present and the universal.

JOAN ZLOTNICK ON POTOK'S BROOKLYN SETTING

Reflecting on his youth, Potok expressed the view that "the compression of urban existence, the living mix of peoples and cultures in my Bronx world, made possible for me a rich variety of culture confrontations."[4] Yet it was Brooklyn, not the Bronx, that Potok chose as the dominant setting for most of his fiction, which might best be described as partly autobiographical.

The shift of locale is understandable, considering the fact that Brooklyn is the home of several well-known Hasidic sects. In dramatizing what he chooses to call the "core-to-core confrontation"[5] experienced by Orthodox Jews reaching out towards new intellectual or aesthetic horizons, Potok undoubtedly recognized that both the confrontation and the "local color" in his fiction would be enhanced by placing the protagonist in conflict not only with his family and his religious heritage, but also with a monolithic Hasidic community. Furthermore, Potok certainly must have felt a connectedness to his tradition since his mother was a direct descendent of one of the great Hasidic dynasties.

Potok's first two novels, *The Chosen* (1967) and *The Promise* (1969), are set in Williamsburg during the 1940's. There had, of course, been a significant Jewish community in Williamsburg prior to this time. Jews had begun to settle there in large numbers at about the time of World War I. Until then, the only Jewish residents had been wealthy German Jewish families, but gradually there developed a community of less affluent Orthodox Eastern European Jews, many of them coming from the Lower East Side, Brownsville, and the Bronx. Soon they were joined by others, mostly Hasidim, fleeing from Nazi persecution and, some years later, by concentration camp survivors.

Notes

4. Chaim Potok, "Culture Confrontation in Urban America: A Writer's Beginnings," in *Literature and the Urban Experience: Essays on the City and Literature*, eds. Michael C. Jaye and Ann Chalmers Watts (New Brunswick, Rutgers University Press, 1981), p. 166.

5. Ibid.

Works by Chaim Potok

The Chosen, 1967.

The Promise, 1969.

My Name is Asher Lev, 1972.

In the Beginning, 1975.

The Jew Confronts Himself in American Literature, 1975.

Wanderings: Chaim Potok's History of the Jews, 1978.

The Book of Lights, 1981.

Davita's Harp, 1985.

Ethical Living for a Modern World: Jewish Insights, 1985.

Theo Tobiasse: Artist in Exile, 1986.

The Gift of Asher Lev, 1990.

I Am the Clay, 1992.

The Tree of Here, 1993.

The Sky of Now: Chronicles of the Slepak Family, 1996.

The Gates of November, 1996.

Zebra and Other Stories, 1998.

My First Seventy-Nine Years: Memoirs of Isaac Stern, 1999.

Old Men at Midnight, 2001.

Annotated Bibliography

Abrams, Alan. "When Cultures Collide." *Jewish News* (Detroit) 22 June 1984, 13ff.

This interview features Potok's views on the film version of *The Chosen*.

Abramson, Edward A. *Chaim Potok*. Boston: Twayne, 1986.

This volume is the first comprehensive critical study of Potok's work, including a strong analysis of themes in *The Chosen*.

Bluefarb, Sam. "The Head, the Heart and the Conflict of Generations in Chaim Potok's *The Chosen*." *College Language Association Journal* June 1971, 402–9.

In his essay, Bluefarb argues that the novel posits that a balance between heart and mind, as embodied by the Malters, is ideal, whereas Danny is "all head."

Field, Leslie. "Chaim Potok and the Critics: Sampler from a Consistent Spectrum." *Studies in American Jewish Literature* 4 (1984): 3–12.

Field provides useful overview of critical reception to Potok's works in this article.

Forbes, Cheryl. "Judaism Under the Secular Umbrella." *Christianity Today* 8 September 1978, 14–21.

Forbes interviews Potok about religion in America in a Christian publication.

Grebstein, Sheldon. "The Phenomenon of the Really Jewish Bestseller: Potok's *The Chosen*." *Studies in American Jewish Literature* Spring 1975, 23–31.

Grebstein discusses the the surprising, mainstream success of Potok's novel, as well as its exploration of the American Dream.

Guttman, Allen. *The Jewish Writer in America: Assimilation and the Crisis in Identity*. New York: Oxford University Press, 1971.

Broad discussion of Jewish-American literature that places Potok's early work within a larger context.

Harap, Louis. *In the Mainstream: The Jewish Presence in Twentieth-Century American Literature, 1950's–1980's*. Westport, CT: Greenwood, 1987: 162–164.

Harap places Potok's early work into a larger literary context in this volume.

Hicks, Granville. "Good Fathers and Good Sons." *Saturday Review* 29 April 1967, 25–26.

In his essay, Hicks discusses the emphasis on father-son relationships in *The Chosen*.

Kremer, Lillian. "Chaim Potok." *Dictionary of Literary Biography*, edited by Daniel Walden, 28:232–43. Detroit: Gale, 1984.

In her biography, Kremer, provides a comprehensive overview of Potok's life and writing career.

Leviant, Curt. "The Hasid as American Hero." *Midstream* November 1967, 76–80.

In his essay, Leviant provides a critical analysis of *The Chosen*.

Lipskar, Mendel. "My Name is Not Asher Lev." *Jewish Affairs* (South Africa) 32 (1977): 31–32.

Lipskar, a rabbi, finds fault with the negative portrait of Hasidism is Potok's first three novels in this essay.

Marovitz, Sanford. "Freedom, Faith, and Fanaticism: Cultural Conflict in the Novels of Chaim Potok." *Studies in American Jewish Literature* 4 (1986): 129–140.

In his essay, Marovitz discusses the conflict that exists between the American dream and ethnic/religious identity for characters in Potok's work.

Nissenson, Hugh. "The Spark and the Shell." *New York Times Book Review* 7 May 1967, 4–5, 34.

In his review, Nissenson argues that *The Chosen*'s gripping plot outshines its sometimes awkward style.

Poll, Solomon. *The Hasidic Community of Williamsburg.* New York: Schocken Books, 1969.

Poll provides a sociological study of the Hasidic communities of Williamsburg in this volume.

Purcell, William F. "Potok's Fathers and Sons." *Studies in American Literature* 26 (1989): 75–92.

In this essay, Purcell gives a thorough, evocative examination of the role of fathers and sons in Potok's fiction.

Rosenfeld, Alvin. "The Progress of the American Jewish Novel." *Contemporary Jewish Review* 7 (1973):115–30.

This article focuses on Jewish American literature since World War II and how Potok played an important role in the genre's evolution.

Shapiro, Karl. "The Necessary People." *Book Week* 23 April 1967, 4, 12.

Shapiro, a poet, discusses *The Chosen* as an allegory.

Shelton, Ken. "Writer on the Roof." *BYU Today* April 1983, 9–11.

Ken Shelton interviews Potok in the Mormon publication.

Sherman, Bernard. Review of *The Chosen. Chicago Jewish Forum* Spring 1968, 215–16.

Like other critics, Sherman finds fault with the novel's style but praises its themes in this interview.

Stampfer, Judah. "The Tension of Piety." *Judaism* Fall 1967, 494–98.

In this famous, oft-quoted review, Stampfer criticizes Potok's portrait of Hasidic life and Freudian psychology while praising his evocation of yeshiva training.

Sternlicht, Sanford. *Chaim Potok: A Critical Companion.* Westport, CN: Greenwood Press, 2000.

Sternlicht provides an updated, comprehensive analysis of Potok's work, including a useful chapter on *The Chosen* that discusses symbols, themes, and a psychoanalytic reading. It also includes an informative chapter on Potok's personal history.

Vanderwerken, David L. "Sport in the Fiction of Chaim Potok (Yeah, Right.)" *Aethlon* 18:2 (Spring 2001): 1–6.

Vanderwerken's is the only article to examine the role of sports in Potok's works.

Walden, Daniel. "Chaim Potok: A *Zwischenmensch* Adrift in the Cultures." *Studies in American Jewish Literature* 4 (1984): 19–25.

Walden discusses how Potok straddles the culture of his religion and the culture of his country.

———, ed. *Conversations with Chaim Potok.* Jackson: University of Mississippi Press, 2001.

This anthology brings together useful interviews that span Potok's career.

"When Culture Confronts Faith: An Interview with Chaim Potok." *College People* October 1983, 8–13.

This Seventh-day Adventist magazine interviews Potok, addressing religion and writing.

Zlotnick, Joan. "The Chosen Borough: Chaim Potok's Brooklyn." *Studies in American Jewish Literature* 4 (1984): 13–18.

Zlotnick focuses on the setting of Potok's novels in this article.

Contributors

Edward A. Abramson has spent a good portion of his career teaching in the Department of American Studies at the University of Hull, and in addition to publishing a number of articles and reviews—and the first comprehensive, book-length analysis on Potok's work—he also wrote books titled *The Immigrant Experience in American Literature* and *Bernard Malamud Revisited*.

Leslie Field taught English at Purdue University and is now a professor emeritus. During her career, she published articles on Chaim Potok, Phillip Roth, and Thomas Wolfe, editing two books on the latter: *Thomas Wolfe's Purdue Speech: Writing and Living*, co-edited by William Braswell, and *The Autobiography of an American Novelist, newly edited versions of The Story of a Novel and Writing and Living*.

Sheldon Grebstein, a past professor at University of Southern Florida, Harpur College, and former president of SUNY-Purchase, has authored a number of academic journal articles and the following books: *Studies in for Whom the Bell Tolls*, *Hemingway's Craft (Crosscurrents: Modern Critiques)*, and *John O'Hara*.

Sanford E. Marovitz spent most of his career teaching English at Kent State University, from which he retired in 1996. Published widely in professional journals and collected volumes of criticism, Marovitz was also co-editor of *Artful Thunder* (1975); collaborated with Clarence Gohdes on the fifth edition of *A Bibliographical Guide to the Study of the Literature of the U.S.A.*; and was the associate editor of the academic journal, *Studies in American Jewish Literature*.

Judah Stampfer is the author of a book of poems, *Jerusalem Has Many Faces*, and a novel, *Sol Meyers*. More recently, he wrote *Fathers and Children*.

Stanford Sternlicht teaches at Syracuse University in both the English Department and the Judaic Studies Program. He's published books on Jean Rhys and James Herriot, and he's contributed articles to a number of periodicals, including *College English, Harvard Magazine, Writer's Digest, Calcutta Review,* and *Renaissance Quarterly.* Sternlicht is also a series editor at Syracuse University Press.

David L. Vanderwerken is a past president of the SLA (Sports Literature Association, perhaps), a regular contributor to *Aethlon,* a sports-themed literary journal, and an avid fisherman who teaches English at Texas Christian University. In addition to a number of academic article publications, Vanderwerken has published the following books: *Faulkner's Literary Children: Patterns of Development; Sport Inside Out: Readings in Literature and Philosophy;* and *Sport in the Classroom: Teaching Sport-Related Courses in the Humanities.*

Daniel Walden, editor of the journal *Studies in Jewish American Literature,* is a professor emeritus of American Studies, English and Comparative Literature at Penn State University. He's authored and edited many books, including critical scholarship on Cynthia Ozick, Bernard Malamud, Chaim Potok, and the role of women in Jewish literature.

Joan Zlotnick teaches English at the Brooklyn College of CUNY. In addition to writing scholarly articles on Kate Chopin and Chaim Potok, she published a book titled *Portrait of an American City: The Novelists' New York.*

Acknowledgments

Chaim Potok, by Edward A. Abramson. © 1986, Twayne Publishers. Reprinted by permission of The Gale Group.

"Chaim Potok and the Critics: Sampler from a Consistent Spectrum" by Leslie Field. From *Studies in American Jewish Literature* 4 (1984): 3–12. Reprinted with permission of *Studies in American Jewish Literature*, Daniel Walden, Editor.

"The Phenomenon of the Really Jewish Bestseller: Potok's *The Chosen*" by Sheldon Grebstein. From *Studies in American Jewish Literature* Spring 1975, 23–31. Reprinted with permission of *Studies in American Jewish Literature*, Daniel Walden, Editor.

"Freedom, Faith, and Fanaticism: Cultural Conflict in the Novels of Chaim Potok" by Sanford Marovitz. From *Studies in American Jewish Literature* 4 (1986): 129–140. Reprinted with permission of *Studies in American Jewish Literature*, Daniel Walden, Editor.

"The Tension of Piety" by Stampfer, Judah. *Judaism* Fall 1967, 494–98. © 1967 by the American Jewish Congress. Reprinted by permission.

Chaim Potok: A Critical Companion, by Sternlicht, Sanford. © 2000 by Greenwood Publishing Group, Inc. Reproduced with permission of Greenwood Publishing Group, Inc., Westport, CT.

"Sport in the Fiction of Chaim Potok (Yeah, Right)" by David L. Vanderwerken. From *Aethlon* 18:2 (Spring 2001) 1–6. This article appeared originally in *Aethlon: The Journal of Sport Literature*. Reprinted with permission.

Index

an unlikely success, 101–102
and war between the Jews in, 23
women as non-existent in, 51
Cold War, 14
Contemporary Jewish Record, 97
"Core-to-Core Cultural confrontation," 117, 119
Counter-culture, 7, 14–15